Your Future in Space

Flip and Debra Schulke
Penelope and Raymond McPhee

Your Future in Space

The U.S. Space Camp® Training Program

foreword by Astronauts
Bruce McCandless and Kathryn D. Sullivan

Design by Robert S. Nemser

Crown Publishers, Inc.
New York

Acknowledgments

A book covering your future in space could not be done without the gifts of both time and creativity from many people.

We are extremely grateful to the U.S. Astronaut Corps as a group and thank especially Astronauts Capt. Bruce McCandless, Kathryn D. Sullivan, Jerry L. Ross and Sherwood C. Spring, who permitted us to photograph many of their training procedures.

From NASA, the following people made possible the NASA photographs used in this book. We thank them for their constant help and for organizing permission for us to photograph at NASA installations.

NASA/Headquarters, Washington, D.C.: Joseph Headlee, Chief, Broadcast and Audio Visual Branch, and Althea Washington, Audio Visual Specialist.

NASA/Johnson Space Center, Houston, Texas: Douglas K. Ward, David B. Alter, L. John Lawrence, Stephen A. Nesbitt and Billie A. Deason. Special thanks to Lisa Vasquez who, at a moment's notice, always finds the photographs that we need; and Wm. F. Moran, Test Director—WETF, who made possible our photographic dives in the underwater training tank.

NASA/Kennedy Space Center, Merritt Island, Florida: Edward K. Harrison, Chief, Television and Field Operations, Gatha F. Cottee, Chief, TV section, Leslie Vock Neihouse and JoAnn Mattey. Extra thanks to Dick Young, Chief, News Center Operations, who has helped us from the early days of the Mercury program at Cape Canaveral.

NASA/Marshall Space Flight Center, Huntsville, Alabama: John B. Taylor, Director of Public Affairs, and David B. Drachlis. Thank you fellow Tektite Aquanaut Charles Cooper, Manager NBS, who enabled us to make our first underwater photographs of astronaut training during the Skylab program through the Shuttle U/W training.

The Space and Rocket Center, Huntsville, Alabama: Edward O. Buckbee, Director, Lee Sentell, Director of Marketing, Rod Collins, Manager, Space Camp, Heiko Einfield, Assistant Manager, Greg Dodwell, Mission Director, Robert Amborski, Mission Director, and Kelly Harrington of Banner Elk, North Carolina, Space Camp Trainee and future astronaut.

To all the above, many, many thanks.

A final "thank you" to our editor at Crown Publishers, Jim Wade, and to Art Director Bob Nemser, a master at combining words and pictures in a meaningful way.

Book and cover design by Robert S. Nemser

Cover—left: Photograph by Astronaut Robert "Hoot" Gibson, NASA. right: Flip & Debra Schulke, copyright © 1986.

All photographs by Flip & Debra Schulke, copyright © 1986, except for the following:
Courtesy NASA, pages: 1, 3, 10, 19, 23, 28, 31-bottom, 33-right, 34-bottom, 36-bottom, 41, 43-right, 44–45, 49, 53, 101-bottom, 104–105, 107, 112–113, 116–117-bottom, 118, 125, 130–131, 132–133, 134.

Page 115-top: Threshold Corporation-copyright © Smithsonian Institution/Lockheed Corporation 1985.

Pages: 120, 122, 123, Courtesy Lockheed Missiles & Space Company, Inc. Sunnyvale, California.

Text copyright © 1986 by Penelope McPhee

Published by Crown Publishers, Inc., 225 Park Avenue South, New York, New York 10003 and represented in Canada by the Canadian MANDA Group

CROWN is a trademark of Crown Publishers, Inc.

Manufactured in Japan

Library of Congress Cataloging-in-Publication Data

Schulke, Flip.
  Your future in space.

  Includes index.
    1. Outer space—Exploration—Popular works.
1. Schulke, Debra. II. McPhee, Penelope Ortner.
III. McPhee, Raymond. IV. Title.
TL793.S328 1986   629.4   86-9003
ISBN 0-517-56418-1

10 9 8 7 6 5 4 3 2 1
First Edition

This book is dedicated to the memory of ten men and women who lost their lives in America's quest for the ultimate frontier . . . space.

Roger Chafee

Virgil Grissom

Gregory Jarvis

Christa McAuliffe

Ronald McNair

Ellison Onizuka

Judith Resnik

Francis Scobee

Michael Smith

Edward White II

"The future doesn't belong to the fainthearted. It belongs to the brave. Nothing ends here. Our hopes and our journeys continue."

President Ronald Reagan,
after the explosion of Challenger,
January 28, 1986

CONTENTS

Foreword

by Bruce McCandless II
Captain, U.S. Navy
NASA Astronaut and
Dr. Kathryn D. Sullivan
NASA Astronaut

My future in space started with the reading, and numerous rereadings, of the book *Rockets, Missiles, and Space Travel,* by the German-born author and educator Willy Ley. The year was 1952. The United States had no "space program." Our country's efforts in rocketry involved launching seized German V-2 rockets in the vicinity of White Sands, New Mexico, using captured German scientists as technical advisors. The concepts presented by Ley captured my mind and imagination. I began seeking out and buying slim books on rocket propulsion, orbital mechanics, and the like. As a junior in high school, I was unable to deal with the calculus involved in the derivation of the equations presented in these books. Consequently, I started buying calculus texts and related mathematical treatises. I was not really successful in teaching myself calculus, but I did stimulate my appetite for later mathematical studies.

The only negative response to my interest in extraterrestrial activities came from my maternal grandfather. Then a retired Navy captain and former United States congressman, his considered opinion was that space travel, while perhaps *theoretically* possible, would certainly not be feasible before the end of the century! I would be better advised to rearrange my priorities and to focus my attention on some more practical goal—something solid such as commanding a battleship, or maybe one of those newfangled aircraft carriers.

After high school I entered the United States Naval Academy, which had been the alma mater of my father and of *both* my grandfathers. In the fall of 1957, my senior year, I and the rest of the world were electrified by the unexpected launch of the Soviet Sputnik I. As seniors, I and my roommates were authorized to have a radio receiver in our room. Ours included several shortwave bands, so we rigged up an illicit outside antenna under cover of darkness and listened. We were rewarded late in the evening with reception of the weak "beep-beep-beep" signal emitted by the first tiny space traveler as it passed overhead.

That event jolted me into the realization that the space age was upon us. Later in the academic year I opted for naval aviation over my other leading choice—submarines. I entered the high-performance jet fighter training "pipeline" in hopes of being well positioned for an astronaut program, should one ever develop. After four years in a carrier-based fighter squadron I was assigned, at my request, to a course

of postgraduate study in electrical engineering at Stanford University. After obtaining a master's degree and embarking on a doctoral course of study, I was surprised by receipt of an invitation to apply for selection as an astronaut. I jumped at the chance—and here I am.

Securing a career position in a space-related field is somewhat like shooting at a moving target; you have to "lead" it rather than aim at its current position. The total scope of space activity is still changing rapidly, so you have to make your own personal forecast of the situation that will exist at the time you are ready to undertake such a career. In this regard it should be stressed that there are at least three major factors influencing the future directions of our country's manned space program: science/technology, money, and politics.

Science and technology define what *can be done,* what *would be beneficial* to do, and approximately *how much it must cost.* The money constraint is a very real one, as space projects must compete with numerous other items for a share of the federal budget. NASA, for example, was unable to simultaneously begin development of *both* the Space Shuttle *and* a space station in the early seventies due to budgetary constraints. Not until January of 1984 did President Reagan authorize the agency to start on a space station. This brings us to the third factor—politics. President Eisenhower created NASA in reaction to the Soviet technological success with Sputnik; President Kennedy committed us to "landing a man on the moon and returning him safely to earth" before the end of the sixties; and President Nixon authorized the start of the Space Shuttle program. It takes that magnitude of national commitment to launch a new manned space program. The time *will* come, however, when private enterprise will undertake significant space projects—and it will come sooner than we dare to think.

The astronaut's role has been aptly compared to the tip of an iceberg. Both are highly visible; both rely on a lot of unseen support. For every astronaut in space there are literally thousands of other space workers involved on the ground as essential members of the team. These include managers, engineers, technicians, scientists, medical personnel, bureaucrats, lawyers, and politicians. They are geographically dispersed at government and industry sites throughout the country and occasionally in foreign locations. It takes every one of these groups of people to make the system operate—and each group offers unique space-related career opportunities to people of differing talents and personal interests.

Space Camp provides a way of living out some of the experiences associated with astronaut training and of broadening your horizons. Lacking a means of building a simulator that can duplicate a space mission with 100 percent fidelity, NASA uses multiple devices to simulate different *portions* of a mission. It is up to the astronaut to mentally "put it all together." In a similar fashion, the Space Camp experience must be appreciated as only a part, albeit a very significant one, of a person's efforts to appreciate the realities of life in space, and to chart a course leading to a satisfying and rewarding career.

Thinking back, I have had two exceptionally memorable moments arising from my activities as an astronaut. One, of course, was the historic first untethered free-flight with the Manned Maneuvering Unit (MMU). This resulted not in excitement, fear, or thrills, but in professional pride and a feeling of relief. Professional pride arose from seeing all of the years of effort by me, by MMU co-developer Ed Whitsett, and by all of the other team members finally bearing fruit in the flawless performance of the MMU in its true environment for the first time. Relief came from finding that no unrelated or exotic problem had cropped up to thwart our carefully laid plans.

The other event revolved around my duties as a CAP-COM or "capsule communicator" during the *Apollo 11* mission, on which the first manned lunar landing was accomplished. I had left the control center just after the landing itself. The crew had a sleep period of several hours scheduled, so I went home to rest before coming on duty for the walk on the lunar surface itself. Well, the crew felt that they would be unable to sleep (little wonder!) so the "walk" was advanced in the timeline and I was telephoned to return. While driving back to the control center, I happened to glance up and see the nearly full moon high in the sky. No matter how hard I tried I could not totally convince myself that there were now *people* on the moon and that I would be talking to and working with them shortly. It was an eerie and vividly remembered feeling of incredulity.

The ability to overcome disbelief, and to function appropriately in spite of it, is an essential part of being an astronaut, of "flying on instruments" in an airplane, and of participating in numerous technical activities of our modern life. Fifty years ago who would have thought that you could sit down in front of a box with wires coming out of it, operate a few switches and knobs, and see and hear other people through the medium of television—in color, no less? Today we routinely thrust our bodies into strange machines for the purposes of taking x-rays and "CAT scans" or receiving radiation therapy. How long will it be before we are able to enter a machine that can "teleport" our bodies to some distant destination at the speed of light? Who will be the first to volunteer for suspended animation—with revival guaranteed by prior extensive testing of laboratory animals?

Preparation for any of these activities involves preparation in many areas. A *technical* education—science, engineering, medicine, or mathematics—is required in order to be a meaningful participant. A *broad* educational background is required in order to be able to assess and to appreciate the consequences of various technological courses of action upon society. Challenging, stimulating activities such as piloting of aircraft, scuba diving, backcountry hiking, etc., also help the participant develop control in stressful situations. Finally, group activities—sports or other "extracurricular" activities—are necessary in order to learn the realities of group dynamics, of leadership, and of subordination of oneself to the achievement of the group objectives.

I would not presume to forecast the future of manned space programs—plural, since the United States will likely have a military manned space program as well as civilian ones (NASA and commercial enterprises). These will take their places along with the Soviet program and various other international participants. The opportunity for international cooperation will be present on a grand scale.

Space is an arena—like the polar regions in the early 1900s—in which success and worldwide prestige can be obtained without the necessity of defeating anyone! It is not a zero-sum game; the fortunes of the human species will prosper as we continually push back the frontiers of space and embark upon new enterprises. There is a lot of truth in the comment that "the science *fiction* of today is the science *fact* of tomorrow." The only unanswered question is "When?" That's up to you. Take today's technological marvels like the Space Shuttle and the Soviet "Mir" space station as "ho-hum" *givens;* use them as foundations upon which to build your own even more advanced human institutions and technological triumphs.

Bruce McCandless II

What will your future be like? Will you be able to live aboard a space base somewhere between the Earth and the Moon? Would you like to be a scientist aboard a Mars-bound interplanetary spaceship? Libraries are full of books describing exciting future space developments like these, and new ones are published every month. But will these dreams really come true someday?

In March of 1985, President Reagan appointed a fifteen-member panel, called the National Commission on Space, to study the future that lies ahead of the United States on the space frontier and identify the toughest challenges and greatest opportunities we face. I had the honor of being included in that group and found our task quite a challenge in its own right. We spent a full year reading reports, receiving testimony from prominent scientists, engineers, business leaders and government officials, and holding hearings before the general public. In the end, I think we came up with a bold and exciting road map for our nation. Those of you who are today in school—grade school through high school—have a very important role to play in this story, because the job of making this vision come true belongs to you!

The scope and pace of space activities will certainly expand in the future, broadening the range of opportunities open to you on this frontier, so it's difficult to choose an exact job description to aim for as you plan your education. Fortunately, there are a few general principles that will steer you well, even if you don't always know where you're going! The story of how I became an astronaut illustrates some of these pretty well.

I first showed an interest in science during the second grade, when my class did a series of simple, fun experiments. The year was 1959. NASA was barely a year old, and the general public heard little, if any, news about space. Science continued to interest me all through elementary school. I can remember reading a very simple book on rocket flight in those early years—the concept of "escape velocity" was especially intriguing to me. Another line of interest was developing at the same time, however, which became the dominant theme of my junior and senior high school studies. Geography and languages attracted most of my curiosity for many years. I wanted to know what other countries were like, both in terms of landscape and climate (physical geography) and people and culture (cultural geography). Learning new languages allowed me to meet these people and cultures on their terms, without the filtering effect of translators or interpreters. I would have given anything to travel to some of the exciting places I read about, but that chance was still many years ahead of me, so I poured all my curiosity into books.

I finished high school, as a language major, in June 1969. Less than one month later, the Apollo 11 lunar module landed on the Moon. Still fascinated by such complex experiments, I watched every available moment of television coverage. It was an unforgettable experience, even as a spectator! Still, "astronaut" in those days was not a career option that school guidance counselors or parents urged on young students—and certainly not one for young women! So, off I went to college, still signed up as a language major.

The University of California at Santa Cruz required that all freshmen take certain "breadth" courses. Basically this meant that I, as a humanities major, had to take three science courses. Two out of three was all it took to reawaken my scientific curiosity and, in my sophomore year, lead me to declare an Earth Sciences major. None of my linguistic or cultural curiosity was wasted, though, as I found this new field offered many chances to travel and many occasions on which it was quite useful to be able to read the scientific papers of European researchers.

I didn't consider space as a career field until I was nearly finished with my doctoral dissertation. At that point, the space shuttle program was still under development and NASA recognized a need for crewmembers who would serve as a mixture of flight engineer and chief scientist. This struck me as analogous to the role I had as a marine geologist aboard oceanic research vessels, so I applied. I also felt that no self-respecting geologist could pass up the chance to see our beautiful planet from such an incredible perspective with her own eyes!

You might well ask why NASA would consider a language major turned marine geologist as a potential astronaut —I wondered about that, too! I had changed career targets several times along the way and had never been directly involved with aerospace engineering, but I had acquired enough important skills and values to qualify for the job. The space jobs of the future will certainly differ in some ways from those of today, but I think a few essential elements will always be keys to success. What are they? They are a combination of personal qualities and educational tools. We will always need people who are curious, self-motivated, self-disciplined, responsible; who are not afraid of hard work and who enjoy the satisfaction of attaining a lofty goal. These are qualities you can begin to develop right now in your schoolwork and other activities. I think they are the main factors that enable you to fulfill your own potential and have a rewarding life, personally and professionally.

As for education specifically, I always looked upon school as my chance to build up a "tool kit" to equip me for a challenging and fun future. To be productive and successful on the space frontier, good "tools" in mathematics, the sciences, engineering, and English will always be important, and not just for the professional scientists and engineers. Our country's future is tied very closely to science and technology in general, so it's also important for our government officials, business people, and the general public to have a good understanding of them.

It's not hard to dream about a bold, exciting future in space and on other worlds, but dreaming alone will not make it true; it will take vision, talent, and dedication. This book tells of a unique camp where many young people are given a taste of the preparation, team work, and satisfaction involved in turning dreams into reality. I hope it whets your appetite for the adventures the future holds for us and motivates you to strive for the highest goals you can set. For me, the greatest personal reward for my efforts was the view of our home planet from a truly amazing perspective. For some of you, the reward may well be a first-hand view of the plains of Mars, as you land to establish a new human outpost. You can be part of a very exciting future!

Kathryn D. Sullivan

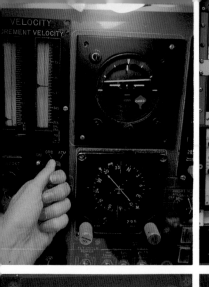

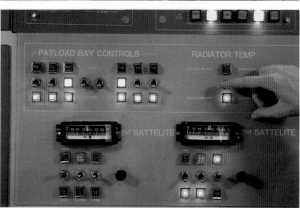

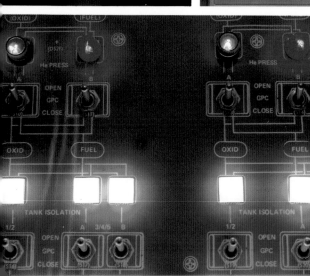
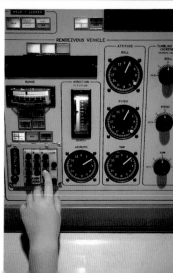

Introduction

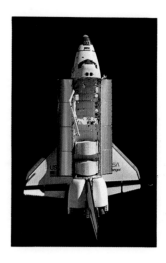

You are poised on the brink of a voyage into the unknown . . . a voyage of exploration into the possibilities and potentials that lie in your own future.

The range of options open to you is as vast as space itself. If current plans and proposals bear fruit, as they seem quite likely to do, the opportunities for you to be personally involved in space are going to expand remarkably in the decades to come. More important, as you make your own contributions in the fields of science and space-age technology, you will become a vital link in the chain of people we need to take us beyond our own planet. As part of our first real space-traveling generation, you'll design spacecraft for interplanetary exploration, occupy space stations and help solve scientific mysteries that have baffled mankind for centuries.

As an example, the National Commission on Space, appointed by President Ronald Reagan, has proposed an extremely ambitious set of long-term goals for space exploration and development. This phased program calls for the establishment of permanent human settlements on the moon by the year 2017, and on Mars just ten years later.

To make these colonies possible, the proposal calls for a series of manned space stations and space ports to be built as a "Highway to Space," leading to and supporting the manned lunar outpost. A similar series of permanent structures then would be built as a "Bridge Between Worlds," forming stepping-stones on the way toward a full-scale base on Mars.

These, in turn, will demand the development of totally new space vehicles and propulsion systems. We will also have to devise techniques to extract minerals and other materials from the lunar surface, from asteroids and from the moons of Mars—and then to process them into useful components in robot-operated space factories.

Highly ambitious proposals of this nature strongly suggest that, if you are interested, it is quite likely that you can play a part in these fascinating developments: either directly as an astronaut, or indirectly as a scientist, engineer or technologist working on the development of the tens of thousands of complex systems that will be needed to achieve our goals in space. Many of you will be the decision makers of the twenty-first century.

If playing a part in the exploration of space appeals to you, an excellent place to begin your training, whatever your age, is the United States Space Camp at Huntsville, Alabama. Outside of the National Aeronautics and Space Administration's own astronaut-training system, it offers the most complete and professional program designed to familiarize potential space explorers with the realities of living and working beyond Earth's atmosphere. Space Camp is a part of the Space and Rocket Center near NASA's Marshall Space Flight Center and has received a substantial amount of educational guidance, as well as actual surplus equipment, from NASA.

Every effort is made to achieve realism in all aspects of the training. "Our aim," says Camp Director Edward O. Buckbee, "is to share with the younger generation the excitement and all the ingredients of space travel."

The camp currently operates three programs: Level I for fifth, sixth and seventh graders; Level II for eighth, ninth and tenth graders and a familiarization program for adults. A rigorous program for advanced students is already on the drawing board.

But, regardless of the trainee's age level, this hands-on program is extremely comprehensive. It includes such varied elements as "astronaut conditioning" at 7:00 each morning, courses in the principles of rocketry and propulsion and training in the techniques of working in zero-gravity, using realistic simulators and mock-ups of Manned Maneuvering Units.

Using the Space Transportation System as an example of the latest development in space technology, the training culminates in an exciting simulated Space Shuttle flight that is carefully based on actual NASA mission profiles.

In this book, we will follow the Space Camp training program, demonstrating the close parallels to actual astronaut training. As you join the astronauts and Space Campers in training, and as you face the challenges of their mission with them, you will learn where your own special areas of interest are within the broad range of possibilities presented by the space program as it is today, and as it will be tomorrow.

And you will be able to form a clearer idea of how to prepare yourself for your future in space.

Space Campers watch astronaut Sherwood Spring suit-up at NASA's Neutral Buoyancy Simulator.

right: Campers Stacy Streuber and Kari Farnham carry out their roles at Mission Control.

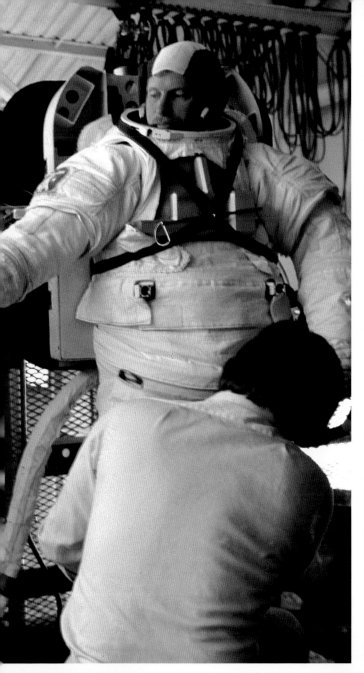

A Space Camper wearing an Apollo-era training suit walks on a copy of the moon's Tranquillity Base.

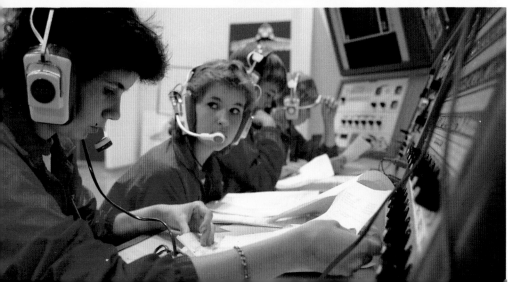

1.
Rocket Power

A History of Rockets and How They Work

The year was 1924. Berlin, the capital of Germany, had partly recovered from the severe shortages and privation that had followed the end of World War I. The fashionable upper-class neighborhood where Wernher von Braun lived was a delightful place for an imaginative and adventurous young boy to grow up.

He was twelve years old when he hit upon the idea of propelling himself at high speed by powering his wagon with skyrockets. He strapped six of the biggest skyrockets he could find to the side of his wagon and ignited them, sending the vehicle out of control down a busy street. After a reprimand by the unamused authorities, he was grounded by his father, Baron von Braun.

That first setback certainly didn't diminish von Braun's interest in rocketry and space travel. His enthusiasm and imagination were

---

left: The original seven astronauts at a Mercury Mission Control panel much simpler than those of today. Left to right: Walter M. Schirra, Jr.; Donald K. (Deke) Slayton; Virgil I. (Gus) Grissom; Chris Craft, Mercury Launch and Mission Director; Gordon L. Cooper; Scott Carpenter; John H. Glenn, Jr.; Alan B. Shepard, Jr.

above: Seven days before his death, President John F. Kennedy inspects the underside of the Saturn One's rocket engines with Dr. Wernher von Braun (director of MSFC and father of Space Camp) on the pad at Cape Canaveral, Florida, during the testing of the Apollo Saturn moon rockets.

fueled by the books of such writers as H. G. Wells and Jules Verne. Encouraged by his mother, an amateur astronomer, his drive and dedication, coupled with an insatiable curiosity about the heavens, led him to become an honor student in physics and mathematics.

By the time he was in his early twenties, von Braun had become an important member of a team of German scientists investigating space travel. His immense ability caught the attention of the German military command, who ordered him to divert his talents to the development of rockets for wartime use. He was stationed at a secret research center at Peenemünde where, prior to and during World War II, he directed programs that ultimately led to development of the V-2—the world's first large rocket that really worked.

As the war drew toward its close, American and Soviet armies raced to be the first to capture the scientific treasures at Peenemünde. Von Braun, acknowledged as Germany's leading rocket scientist, led his team of 117 scientists to the West, where they ultimately encountered and surrendered to American forces. Von Braun was only thirty-five at the time.

Thus, they brought their advanced scientific knowledge to the United States, where they continued working on their rockets with a single purpose—space travel.

Today, when you arrive at Space Camp in Huntsville, adjacent to the Alabama Space and Rocket Center, the spirit of Wernher von Braun is never far away. It was here at the Marshall Space Flight Center, under his guidance, that America's space program began. Here, he and his Peenemünde team developed the rockets that put the first satellite in orbit, sent men to the moon and power today's Space Shuttle.

The entire history of America's manned space program was preserved by von Braun himself, when he created the Space and Rocket Center in Huntsville, Alabama. One day, nearly sixty years after his abortive attempt to turn his wagon into a rocket ship, he walked through the museum he had created and said to his companion, "Why don't we encourage study in aerospace and science just like pro football and tennis players promote their sports?" He had envisioned both a need and an opportunity for the kind of exciting exposure to space technology that would inspire young people and prepare them to fulfill their potential in the exploration of space. The same mind that developed the Saturn rocket had given birth to Space Camp.

So today, as you don your space suit to begin your astronaut training, you find yourself surrounded by the rockets that are Dr. von Braun's legacy . . . from an early Redstone to the massive Saturn V that launched men on their way to the moon.

Building Your Own Model Rocket

The first project on your Space Camp agenda is the basic theory of rocket propulsion and the history of America's manned space program.

In its simplest form, a rocket is an unmanned craft with a propulsion system, a source of fuel and a guidance system, which can be as simple as a set of tail fins. Although small rockets were fired by the ancient Chinese, the fundamental principles of getting the rocket off the ground were defined by Sir Isaac Newton three hundred years ago. Newton's complete Laws of Motion, encompassed in three basic laws, was so perfect that it remains nearly intact to this day.

opposite page: The first manned orbital flight by the United States with astronaut John Glenn onboard the "Friendship 7" Mercury 6. Glenn completed three orbits in 4 hours 55 minutes on February 20, 1962.

above: Apollo 17 was the sixth and last manned lunar landing, bringing home 243 pounds of lunar samples gathered with the Lunar Roving Vehicle. Here, Eugene Cernan checks out the LRV prior to loading the vehicle with equipment during his EVA on December 11, 1972. The mountain in the right background is the South Massif.

left: Space Camp trainee Dacia Jessick sits in an engineering model of the LRV —Lunar Roving Vehicle (also called the moon buggy)—while wearing an Apollo-era training EVA suit.

Space Camp trainees, prepared for launch in an Apollo flight deck training capsule, lie on their backs just as the astronauts did.

Newton's Laws allow us to predict the forces that will come into play when two bodies interact. Building your own model rocket is an excellent way to try out Newton's theory firsthand. At Space Camp, trainees learn that the combination of fuel and oxidizer mixed in a combustion chamber provides thrust through the exhaust. When the engine is activated, the fuel ignites and burns and the exhaust rushes out the rear. This thrust is Newton's "equal and opposite force" that sends the vertical rocket toward the sky.

Using kits, campers assemble their own rockets, paying careful attention to detail in order to determine the size and placement of the fins that will guide the rocket. A bee or cricket placed in the nose cone performs the role of astronaut. These creatures also voyage into space as part of Spacelab and Space Shuttle experiments.

Five . . . four . . . three . . . two . . . one . . . . Fire! The sudden hiss of ignition is accompanied by a flash of smoke as the small craft races skyward. Suddenly, a tiny parachute bursts open, carrying the "cricketnaut" gently back to Earth. The insects are sent aloft for a purpose. Their ability to jump or fly normally will be tested after their flight.

The history of rocketry has centered around building bigger and more powerful rockets capable of carrying larger loads farther. Today, the power required to launch the Space Shuttle beyond the Earth's atmosphere is nearly enough to light the entire eastern seaboard of the United States for the period of the burn.

Nowhere can you see development of rocketry illustrated more graphically than at Space Camp, where the skyline is dominated by giant missiles surrounded by their smaller predecessors.

The Race for Space

When the Soviet Union launched the first artificial satellite in October 1957, the race for space began. Fearful of the military advantage that Sputnik gave the Soviets, the United States government formed NASA and made manned space flight its number one priority.

Mercury

NASA's first manned project was the Mercury program, which lasted from 1958 to 1963. Its stated objectives were to orbit a manned spacecraft around the Earth; to study man's ability to function in space and to recover both man and spacecraft safely. Its number one goal was to get a man into space before the Russians. The names of the seven test pilots who were chosen to be our first astronauts are a roll call of America's space pioneers: Alan B. Shepard, Jr., Virgil I. Grissom, John H. Glenn, Jr., M. Scott Carpenter, Walter M. Schirra, Jr., L. Gordon Cooper, Jr., and Donald K. Slayton became national heroes even before their first flight.

Alan Shepard became the first American in space on May 5, 1961, when he made a 15-minute and 22-second suborbital flight, but Russian cosmonaut Yuri Gagarin actually became the first person to enter space when he orbited the Earth on April 21, 1961. The propulsion system for the suborbital Mercury flights was the single-stage Redstone rocket, which had been developed originally as a military ballistic missile. John Glenn became the first American to orbit Earth on February 20, 1962. Mercury's orbital flights were propelled by the Atlas rocket.

Gemini

In a special message to Congress on May 25, 1961, President John F. Kennedy set forth the goal of America's second manned space program. It was nothing less than the achievement of one of humanity's oldest dreams—to land a man on the moon. The first stage of the project was named Gemini for its two-man crew. Its objectives were to subject men and equipment to

On July 20, 1969, Apollo 11 crew member Neil Armstrong's first words upon stepping on the surface of the moon were: "That's one small step for a man, one giant leap for mankind." Shortly thereafter Armstrong took this picture of Buzz Aldrin. This was the first manned lunar landing ever.

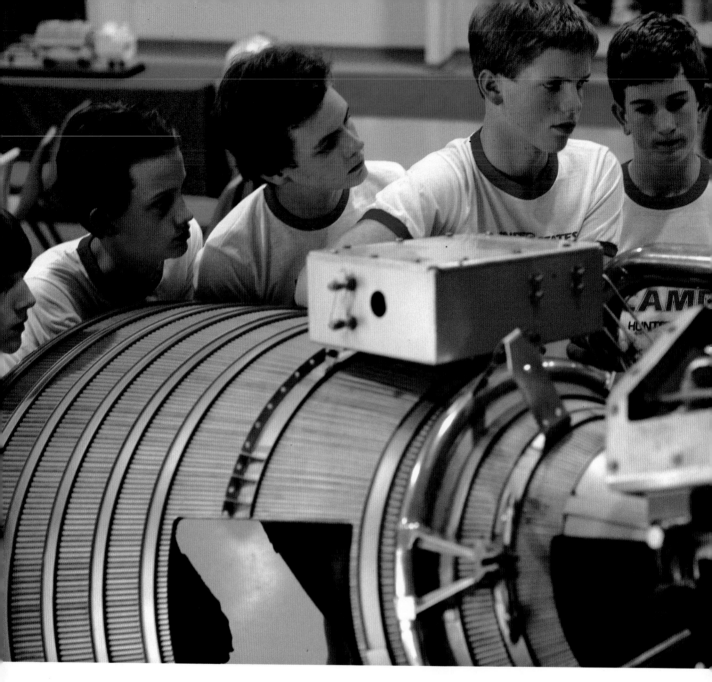

above: One of von Braun's original rocket team engineers, and a propulsion engineer at NASA until his retirement, Konrad Dannenberg explains the differences between the shuttle's engines and this RL 10 rocket engine used for going to the moon.

right: Model rockets are built and launched with a live "payload specimen" to see if the specimen, a bee, survives the rigors of the launch's g forces. This trainer finds that one specimen of his payload did not survive lift-off, while the other clings to the top for dear life!

space flights of up to two weeks' duration; to rendezvous and dock with other orbiting vehicles and to maneuver the docked combination by using the target vehicle's propulsion systems and to perfect methods of reentering the Earth's atmosphere and landing at a preselected site on land. The larger Titan II rocket was used for propulsion of the heavier capsule. During Gemini IV, in June 1965, astronaut Ed White became the first man ever to walk in space, and on March 16, 1966, Gemini VIII accomplished the first docking with another space vehicle.

Apollo

"One small step for man; one giant step for mankind." The words of Neil A. Armstrong, commander of Apollo 11, on July 20, 1969, when he became the first man ever to walk on the moon, expressed the pride of every American. Apollo had accomplished its primary goal—to land Americans on the moon and return them safely to Earth. The Apollo program ultimately accomplished its further goals of achieving preeminence in space for the United States; carrying out a program of scientific exploration of the moon; developing man's capability to work in the lunar environment and creating the technology to meet other national interests in space.

The propulsion system for Apollo, the two-stage Saturn IB and the three-stage Saturn V, were the first nonmilitary rockets specifically designed for manned space flight.

The Apollo missions placed a total of twelve American astronauts on the surface of the moon, where they performed or emplaced a number of scientific experiments, explored sizable areas of the lunar surface, collected geological samples and, incidentally, awed hundreds of millions of viewers around the world with live television pictures of the most momentous achievement in the history of human endeavor.

Skylab

America's first experimental space station, Skylab, was launched May 14, 1973, using the Apollo-Saturn hardware and design. Despite some early mechanical difficulties, Skylab proved that man could live and work in space for extended periods of time and helped us expand our knowledge of solar astronomy well beyond Earth-based observations. Three three-man crews occupied Skylab for a total of 171 days 13 hours. Skylab remained in orbit for more than six years, completing 34,981 orbits.

Apollo-Soyuz

The Apollo-Soyuz project was the first international manned spaceflight. In July 1975, an American and Soviet spacecraft rendezvoused and docked, opening the way for international space rescue as well as for future joint manned flights.

The Shuttle Era

Apollo was a spectacular milestone in space exploration. But each mission remained a single, one-time-only occurrence—and an expensive one at that. On January 5, 1972, President Richard M. Nixon announced that NASA would proceed with the development of a reusable low-cost space shuttle that would "take the astronomical costs out of astronautics." The Space Transportation System (STS), popularly known as the Space Shuttle, permits space crews to use the same craft again and again. The possibility of regular, frequent flights would, according to President Nixon, turn "the space frontier of the 1970s into familiar territory." The Space Shuttle heralded a new space age—of which you are about to become a part.

Trainees learn the principles of rocket propulsion by building their own rockets and launching them with a live payload (bee or cricket).

2. The Space Shuttle

Getting to Know Your Spacecraft

Before you begin your Space Camp shuttle mission, you'll undergo an intensive period of training. Like the astronauts themselves, you'll need to begin with a complete understanding of all aspects of the craft that will carry you to space and become your home beyond the boundaries of the Earth.

NASA's Space Shuttle is the world's first true aerospace vehicle—equally at home in space and in the atmosphere. It is also the first spaceflight system that can be reused. Not unlike earlier launch vehicles, it delivers cargoes to space. But, uniquely, it is also capable of returning them to Earth. Its versatile design lets it take off like a rocket, behave in space like a spacecraft, guided by reaction thrusters, and fly in Earth's atmosphere and gravity like an airplane.

The Space Shuttle will be the backbone of

the United States space efforts for much of the rest of this century. The major portion of our space exploration and development will be dependent on its efficiency and reliability. It will allow us to build and maintain a permanent manned space station; make repairs on orbiting satellites and other equipment; perform scientific investigation in space and build the bases from which we will fly manned probes to other planets. Thus, the Space Shuttle is the primary building block of *your* future in space.

On April 12, 1981, exactly twenty years to the day after Soviet cosmonaut Yuri Gagarin became the first man in space, astronauts John Young and Robert Crippen successfully flew the first test flight of the shuttle. In their orbiter Columbia, they were launched from the Kennedy Space Center at Cape Canaveral, Florida, and two days later landed at Edwards Air Force Base in California. No unmanned test flights of the shuttle had preceded the mission. This was the first time in NASA's history that astronauts had been launched in a new space vehicle on its first flight.

Space Shuttle Orbiters

Enterprise (OV-101)
The first orbiter spacecraft built as a test vehicle and not intended for space flight. Rolled out September 17, 1976.

left: Inside the Vehicle Assembly Building (VAB), the orbiter is raised to a vertical position where it will be mated with the SRBs and the ET. It is then ready for rollout to the launch pad. The VAB is one of the largest buildings in the world: 525 feet tall, with a ground area of 8 acres.

above: The assembled shuttle is rolled out to launch complex pad 39-A on the huge Mobile Launching Platform. Both are being carried to the pad on the Crawler Transporter from the VAB on a roadway 130 feet wide— as wide as an 8-lane highway—for 3.5 miles.

Columbia (OV-102)

First flight orbiter. Rolled out March 8, 1979. First flight STS-1, April 12–14, 1981. Also used for STS-2 through 5 and STS-9, the first Spacelab mission.

Challenger (OV-099)

Second operational orbiter. Rolled out June 30, 1982. First flight ST-6, April 4–9, 1983. On January 28, 1986, on its tenth mission, Challenger exploded seventy-two seconds after lift-off. The seven crew members, who perished in the explosion, were: commander Francis R. Scobee, pilot Michael J. Smith, mission specialists Judith Resnik, Ronald McNair and Ellison Onizuka, payload specialist Gregory Jarvis and teacher Christa McAuliffe.

Discovery (OV-103)

The third operational orbiter. Rolled out October 16, 1983. First flight STS-41D, August 30–September 5, 1984. On its third mission, the Discovery crew retrieved two satellites that had become inoperable. On its fifth mission, Discovery carried Utah Senator Jacob Garn to space.

Atlantis (OV-104)

The fourth operational orbiter. Rolled out April 6, 1985. In its maiden voyage, October 3–7, 1985, Atlantis conducted a secret Defense Department mission.

The Mission Crew

The Space Shuttle orbiter, in which you will train at Space Camp, is an almost exact simulation of the actual orbiters. NASA's orbiters can accommodate eight people on flights lasting up to thirty days. Crew positions include commander, pilot, mission specialists and payload specialists. The commander and pilot fly the orbiter. Mission specialists are trained astronauts who are normally also skilled in payload operations. Mission specialists carry out operations directly related to the spacecraft and assist the payload specialists with scientific or technical investigations. One to four payload specialists, who are not usually astronauts, may be assigned to the flight to carry out scientific or technical experimentation or to operate specialized equipment in orbit. As you proceed with your mission training, you'll learn more about the functions of these crew members and the training required for each role. During your Space Camp training, you'll have an opportunity to participate both on the mission control team and as a crew member.

The Parts of Your Space Shuttle

The shuttle orbiter, which carries the crew and payload into space, is the principal part of the shuttle. It is a reusable workhorse designed to last for one hundred flights. About the size and general shape of a DC-9 commercial jet airplane, the orbiter is part aircraft and part spacecraft. The orbiter in which you will carry out your space mission measures 122 feet (37 meters) long and 57 feet (17 meters) high with a wingspan of 78 feet (24 meters). Although it looks much like an airliner with the wings located toward the rear, the Space Shuttle is in fact more like a space truck. It is principally designed to carry cargo—not people—into space, and although the shuttle flights are intended to occur frequently, they are not yet routine.

The center of the orbiter's fuselage is dominated by a 15-by-60-foot cargo bay for carrying payloads. Forward of the cargo bay is the crew compartment that would be your home during a real space mission. Aft or rear of the cargo bay are the three Space Shuttle Main Engines (SSMEs) that propel the orbiter during launch.

These engines, with a major assist from the Solid Rocket Boosters (SRBs), are used to take you and your orbiter to the edge of space. The most advanced liquid-fuel rockets ever built, each of the main engines can produce 383,900 pounds (1.6 million newtons) of thrust at sea level. In the vacuum of space, they can produce 470,000 pounds (2 million newtons). These engines can burn for about eight minutes and draw an astonishing flood of 64,000 gallons of propellant fuel each minute.

On the launchpad, the orbiter is mated to two solid rocket boosters and a giant external fuel tank. The assembled shuttle weighs about 4.5 million pounds (2 million kilograms) at lift-off.

above: The protective outer shell of the orbiter consists of highly heat-resistant "tiles." This resistance is demonstrated by holding a hot flame to a tile, then touching the tile. It's not hot!

left: The shuttle's exterior is covered by nearly 32,000 heat-resistant tiles that protect the craft from the more than 2,300-degree heat generated during reentry. Almost no two tiles are alike. Here, damaged or missing tiles on Columbia are replaced.

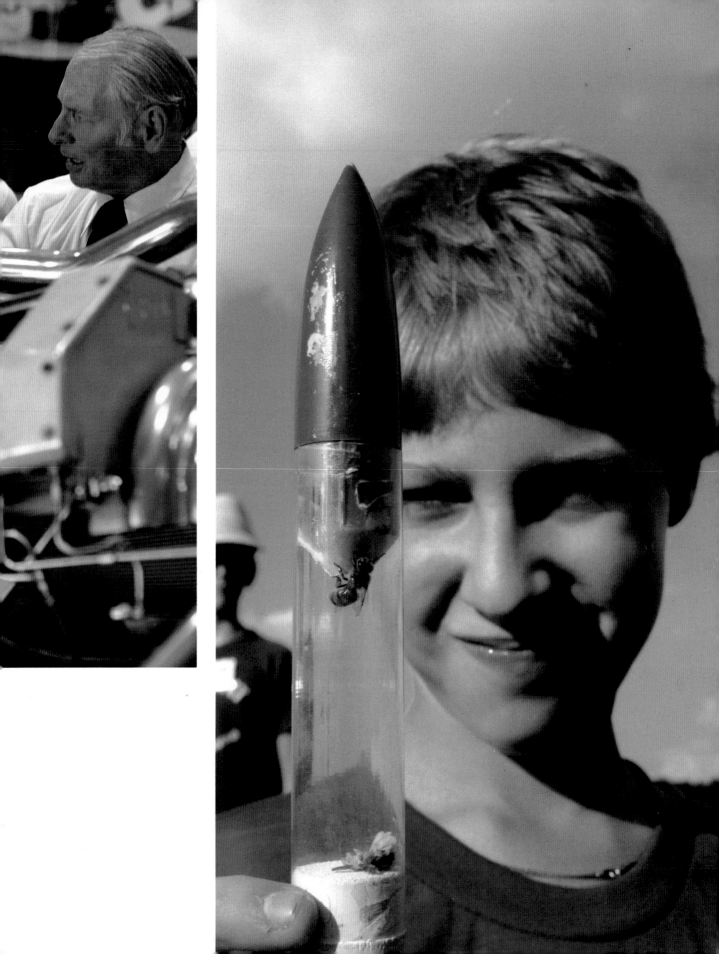

above: Commander Paul Shanley, left, and pilot Kelly Harrington at the Space Camp shuttle flight deck console ready for launch.

right: During a training session in the Columbia's cabin at KSC, STS-1 commander John Young, left, and pilot Robert L. Crippen give the thumbs-up sign.

The shuttle's two SRBs help lift the assemblage away from Earth's gravitational pull. They provide most of the power to lift the shuttle off the launchpad and propel it during the first two minutes of flight. The SRBs contain a solid propellant composed of a mixture of aluminum powder, aluminum perchlorate powder and a dash of iron oxide catalyst held together with a polymer binder. They each produce 2.6 million pounds (11.8 million newtons) of thrust at lift-off. Together with the three main engines on the orbiter, this gives the shuttle a total lift-off thrust of 6.5 million pounds (28.9 million newtons).

After the propellants are consumed, the solid rocket boosters separate from the shuttle. Borne by parachutes, they fall into a predetermined area of the ocean where they are retrieved for future use.

The huge External Fuel Tank (ET) attaches to the belly of the orbiter and feeds propellants to the orbiter's main engines throughout the ascent into near-orbit. Made of aluminum, this external tank is 154 feet long and 28½ feet in diameter. At lift-off it weighs more than 1.5 million pounds. The external tank feeds liquid oxygen and hydrogen from two inner tanks to the main engines. The external tank is the only part of the launch configuration that is not reused. After lift-off, just short of reaching final orbit, the tank separates and drops back to Earth, falling into an uninhabited stretch of the Indian Ocean. However, a great deal of thought is being given to techniques whereby external fuel tanks might be left in a shallow parking orbit around the Earth, rather than being destroyed after each mission. After all, these tanks contain a substantial amount of aluminum and other raw materials that would be useful if they were available in space. In addition, without significant remanufacturing, the tanks could provide an excellent micrometeorite shield for space station components.

The Orbital Maneuvering System (OMS) engines, with 6,000 pounds of thrust, supply the last increment of velocity to reach orbit. You will also use them for in-orbit and de-orbit maneuvers. They burn nitrogen tetroxide for the oxidizer and monomethyl hydrazine for fuel.

The orbiter carries its cargo in a huge payload bay. The bay is versatile enough to accommodate all sizes and shapes of unmanned spacecraft, as well as fully equipped laboratories such as Spacelab. The shuttle's performance is being improved to the point where it eventually will be able to carry a payload weight of 65,000 pounds.

The shuttle orbiter is divided into five sections: the forward fuselage, midsection fuselage, aft fuselage, vertical stabilizer and wings. Most of the structure is made of aluminum. Because it must withstand both the thrust and the high temperatures of the engines, the aft section is constructed of a lightweight, high-strength composite of titanium and boron-epoxy.

Thermal control is a vital part of the successful operation of any spacecraft. During launch, and especially during reentry into the Earth's atmosphere, the outer surface of your spacecraft is subjected to radically high temperatures. Unlike earlier space vehicles, the shuttle needs a protection system that is reusable, lightweight and durable. This system also functions as the aerodynamic skin of the orbiter.

The shuttle's unique Thermal Protection System (TPS) is an important feature in its reusable design. Every part of the shuttle's external shell is shielded by some type of thermal protection. Rigid silica tiles protect the areas that encounter intense heat when the orbiter reenters the Earth's atmosphere. The white tiles that cover the upper and forward fuselage and the tops of the wings can absorb and dissipate temperatures as high as 1200° F. (650° C.). The black tiles on the underside of the orbiter can absorb even higher temperatures, reaching 2300° F. (1260° C.). The areas that receive the most heat on reentry, such as the nose and leading edges of the wings, are covered with black panels made of Reinforced Carbon Carbon (RCC). These panels are capable of absorbing temperatures in excess of 2800° F. (1535° C.). Every one of the 32,000 tiles that covers the Space Shuttle must be installed by hand. Each tile has an individual serial number that is stored in a computer, along with information on its exact size and the curvature of the surface it

above: Behind the commander and pilot, the rest of the crew awaits lift-off. Mission specialists in the first row, payload specialists in the second. In the center is the circular airlock tunnel that leads to the Spacelab. Payload displays and controls for satellite launches are above the airlock.

left: STS-61C crew members simulate a launch mode wearing Anti-G suits to prevent blackouts and Launch and Entry Helmets. Front, left to right: Charles F. Bolden, pilot, Robert (Hoot) Gibson, commander. Rear stations, left to right: mission specialists George D. Nelson and Steven A. Hawley.

right: Payload Specialist Rob Reider, wearing his Launch and Entry Helmet, checks a motion sensor monitor during launch.

Astronaut Mission Specialist Bruce McCandless checks the MMU he will be using on mission 41-B to make the first untethered space walk. The MMU is in its cradle inside the payload bay of the Challenger, where it will ride until McCandless takes it out for his EVA.

is designed to protect. Should a tile be damaged in flight, technicians need only call up the correct serial number, and a perfectly configured replacement tile will be delivered to them.

The upper payload bay doors, as well as the mid and aft sides of the fuselage are covered with a Flexible Reusable Surface Insulation (FRSI). This material, which resembles a quilt, is tougher, lighter and cheaper than the tiles. It replaces most of the white tile areas on the orbiters Discovery and Atlantis.

Living Quarters

Whether you are a commander, pilot, mission specialist or payload specialist, your living quarters on board the actual shuttle would be in the orbiter's crew compartment, which has three decks. The flight deck on top contains the flight controls and crew stations for launch, orbit and landing. The second level, the mid-deck, houses accommodations for eating, sleeping and hygiene. The equipment bay on the bottom deck is a storage area and contains parts of the waste-disposal and life-support systems.

The shuttle is roomy enough to be quite comfortable for its seven- to eight-person crew. The flight crew, including commander, pilot and mission specialists, sit in the upper level of the flight deck. The passengers take-off seats are in the lower level of the forward cabin. The passengers may either be people connected with payload experiments or observers. This lower section also has space for three "rescue" seats that can be used for extra passengers in an emergency. It is possible, for example, that another ship could break down and have to be abandoned in space. In such an event, the shuttle could rescue the crew and return them safely to Earth.

Environmental Control and Life Support

Unlike the astronauts who manned earlier spacecraft, you'll be able to live and work aboard the shuttle in a shirt-sleeve environment. The orbiter's Environmental Control and Life Support System (ECLSS) maintains the temperature at 61° to 90° F. The system also pressurizes the crew compartment with a breathable mixture of 21 percent oxygen and 79 percent nitrogen, keeping

A Space Camp payload specialist punctures his finger for a blood sample used to conduct a blood glucose test during his mission in the Spacelab.

left: MIT's Byron Lichtenberg, a payload specialist onboard Spacelab 1, refers to his checklist on the life sciences rack.

During mission 41-C, the eleventh flight of the shuttle, Mission Specialist James (Ox) van Hoften uses his MMU to return to the flight deck after repairing the injured Solar Maximum satellite. The "Solar Max" is visible in its dock at the aft end of the payload bay. It was "captured" by the RMS arm (right) operated by Terry J. Hart inside the aft flight deck.

toxic gases below harmful levels. The system stores water for drinking and personal hygiene, as well as for cooling the spacecraft. It also functions to process crew waste in a sanitary manner.

Power Generation

The orbiter has one system to supply electrical power and another to supply hydraulic power. Electrical power is generated by three fuel cells that use cryogenically stored hydrogen and oxygen reactants. Three independent hydraulic pumps powered by this electricity provide hydraulic power.

The Cargo Bay

The lower level of the forward cabin contains an airlock, or hatch, through which crew members crawl to get outside the ship or into the cargo bay. Such an operation outside the cabin is called an Extravehicular Activity (EVA). Your Space Camp mission will require specific training in EVAs.

Long doors run the entire length of the cargo bay. They are usually opened wide to give the crew access to the payload. Special radiators in the cargo-bay doors control the buildup of heat in the orbiter. As soon as you're in orbit, you must open the two curved cargo-bay doors. Otherwise, heat will build up inside the orbiter and you'll be forced to land prematurely. You'll have to close the doors again just before retrofire.

The Remote Manipulator System (RMS) or payload handler is a mechanical arm in the cargo-bay area. A payload specialist can control this arm using the flight controls on the flight deck of the craft. The fifty-foot arm has three joints similar to a shoulder, an elbow and a wrist. Its hand is called an end effector. Video cameras enable you to watch the arm's movement on TV monitors. You'll use the RMS for launching and retrieving satellites, as well as for repairs.

Spacelab

One of the primary purposes of the shuttle flights has been to carry Spacelab into orbit and return it safely to Earth. As its name implies, Spacelab is a laboratory designed for use in space. When this self-contained lab is placed inside the shuttle's cargo bay, it converts the shuttle into a ver-

Space Camp EVA repair work being done on the Spacelab pallet.

Astronaut James D. van Hoften, 51-I
mission specialist, is photographed through
Discovery's overhead windows after the
Syncom 1V-3 satellite was released. Van
Hoften is in the foot restraint at the end
of the RMS arm where he was repairing
the satellite.

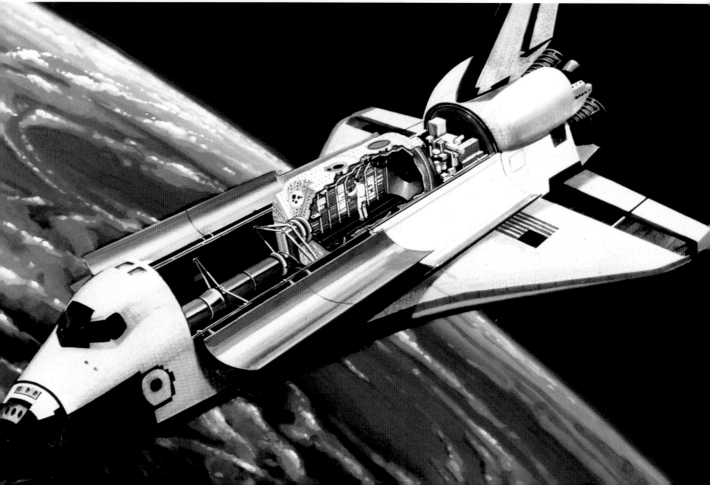

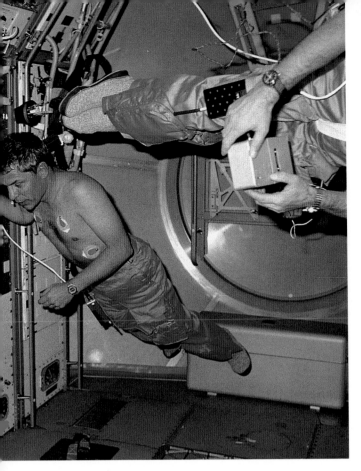

top left: The orbiter Columbia makes its final turn before touching down on the runway.

above: Mission Specialist Robert A. R. Parker works in the Spacelab while floating weightlessly on STS-9, Spacelab-1. Some of the main objectives of this mission were studying the physiological effects of weightlessness and understanding the problems of motion sickness (SAS).

left: Cutaway drawing of shuttle showing Spacelab in cargo bay.

satile orbital research facility. It is, in effect, a temporary space station, complete with computers, scientific measuring instruments and equipment for conducting all sorts of experiments in space. Those of you who are training for scientific careers in space will have an opportunity at Space Camp to perform experiments in Spacelab.

Spacelab is an important step in international space exploration. It was developed by the European Space Agency (ESA) to be part of our Space Transportation System (STS). Spacelab can be used by scientists from countries around the world. Its potential benefits are nearly limitless. The reusable laboratory is already conducting wide-ranging experiments in such fields as life sciences, plasma physics, astronomy, high-energy astrophysics, solar physics, atmospheric physics, materials sciences and Earth observations.

Data Processing

Five onboard computers handle the data processing during your shuttle flight. The computers are capable of working independently or together. They check on one another and even vote if they disagree. The system also has multiplex-demultiplexers to translate signals to and from the orbiter's systems and sensors into computer language. Various display panels show you what is happening and let you communicate with the system.

Now that you're familiar with the physical structure of your spacecraft, you're ready to begin your training to live in space.

3.
Gravity

Zero-Gravity, G-Forces and Weightlessness

Perhaps the most unusual, intriguing and frustrating set of phenomena that you will encounter on your voyage beyond the boundaries of the Earth is the way in which the physics of space travel alter and distort the effects of gravity.

For every moment of your life you have experienced, dealt with and compensated for Earth's normal gravity. Every movement you have ever made has involved a subconscious calculation about the effect of gravity on your action. Now, from the instant that your Space Shuttle's giant engines ignite until your wheels stop rolling at touchdown, all the rules of motion, direction, weight and orientation will change.

Learning to understand the effects of increased g-forces during lift-off and landing and, even more important, how to cope with the weightlessness you will experience throughout

---

left: In the shuttle's payload bay simulator, astronaut Bruce McCandless propels himself forward using an MMU specially designed to work in water exactly as it would in the weightlessness of space, during mission training at JSC's WET-F pool.

above: After watching astronauts simulating EVAs in the weightless environment of water (at MSFC's NBS), a camper has a chance to do the same in a swimming pool. His feet held in foot restraints, he changes a film canister on the exterior of a Skylab mock-up.

your flight, will be a major element in your astronaut training at Space Camp.

Increased G-Forces

During launch and landing, the relative change in speed of your Space Shuttle as it accelerates or decelerates will cause you to feel heavier. Your body will be pushed back or down into your seat, as if the force of gravity has, for a brief period of time, become greater.

The effect of this force is measured in gravitational units called g-forces. Your normal weight on earth is 1 g. Accelerating to 2 g makes you feel as if your weight has doubled. The Space Shuttle's maximum acceleration is 3 g—only a fraction of the 6 to 9 g experienced during launch by the Apollo astronauts.

At the point of peak acceleration during a shuttle launch, you will feel as if a great, soft weight is pressing on your body. You will be able to move your arms to perform essential navigational tasks, but it will require a substantial effort.

Because the force that is causing the acceleration is coming from the shuttle's engines at the rear of the craft, the g-forces will press you backward, into your seat. Your body is able to handle moderate g-forces in this direction quite easily, and you will experience no disorientation or other serious adverse effects.

The effect of g-forces during landing is somewhat different. As the orbiter descends through the atmosphere, it loses speed rapidly. The deceleration during entry is only about 1.5 g but, because the shuttle is now oriented roughly parallel to the Earth's surface, this force is experienced as if the increased weight were pressing down on you from above.

Blood is forced away from your brain and toward the lower parts of your body. If your brain is deprived of too great a portion of its necessary blood supply, you can partially lose consciousness (grayout) or pass out completely (blackout). Obviously, any loss of mental ability during the critical landing period must be avoided. So you will wear an anti-g suit that is very similar to the garment worn by pilots of high-performance jet fighters. The suit has pressure bladders that surround your lower body and legs. As g-forces increase, the bladders are inflated to squeeze blood back into your upper torso, where it is more readily available to nourish your brain.

The Effects of Weightlessness

A much more extraordinary departure from the gravitational norm you are used to occurs while the spacecraft is in orbit. This is the experience of weightlessness—the total suspension of the gravitational pull on your body and on all the objects you come in contact with.

We've all seen photographs and television pictures of astronauts living and working in a weightless state. They accomplish seemingly impossible gymnastic feats without apparent effort, chase an errant globule of orange juice around their quarters with a straw or, with total unconcern, perform their mission assignment while hanging suspended from the "ceiling" of their craft.

It looks like a lot of fun, and actually it is. But the condition of zero-gravity also poses problems, challenges and opportunities that you must understand and be prepared to deal with if you hope to live and work successfully in space.

To grasp why weightlessness occurs, you first need to know something about orbital mechanics —the process that keeps your Space Shuttle circling the globe without any thrust from its engines.

In essence, orbit is achieved when two opposing forces are balanced. Left unchecked after lift-off, the orbiter would continue in a straight line into space. This property is called inertia, and relates to Newton's First Law. However, the orbiter doesn't speed off into space because Earth's gravity is pulling it down. When these two forces of inertia and gravity are equal, they counteract each other precisely, so your orbiter will neither fly off into outer space nor will it fall back to the ground. It will simply hang there, constantly "falling" around the Earth.

Gravitational force becomes stronger the closer an object is to the Earth. Therefore, the speed that is needed to match gravity's pull and establish an orbit varies with the height of the orbit desired. To attain a relatively low orbit of about 150 miles, the Space Shuttle needs to reach a speed of approximately 17,500 mph. By contrast, a communications satellite in a geosynchronous orbit over the Equator has an orbital altitude of 22,240 miles, but it requires a speed of only 6,875 mph to maintain its position.

The same balancing of forces that neutralizes Earth's gravitational pull on your orbital vehicle eliminates their effect on all the orbiter's contents . . . including you! As a result, you and your spacecraft are falling together, at the same speed and in the same direction. This fact negates any gravitational relationship between you, the spacecraft and any other objects in it, and causes the condition we call weightlessness.

Living and Working in Zero-G

Most of the intensive zero-g training you will receive at Space Camp is designed to familiarize you with the problems of working in a weightless condition and to teach you how to overcome the difficulties involved.

While increased g-forces are easy to simulate

Astronauts William and Anna Fisher "float" in the weightlessness experienced for one minute during a parabolic arc flown by a KC-135 aircraft. They were married to each other before being selected into the astronaut corps.

The camp trainee experiences astronaut
training on the multi-axis simulator.
Trainees must learn to perform tasks
while in a state of disorientation as the
multi-axis seat pitches, yaws and rolls.

Using the 5 degrees of freedom (5-DF) simulator gives the trainee freedom of movement in five directions—side motion, left, right, up, down, and across the floor—on air bearings, simulating weightlessness.

Greg Galperin experiences the unusual sensation of "the moon hop." Springs remove five-sixth's of a person's weight, leaving one-sixth (simulating the gravity of the moon) and giving a light, weightless freedom of movement. The astronauts hopped on the moon because it was easier than walking—and faster.

during training, the effects of zero-gravity are much more difficult to duplicate. Unfortunately, no one has yet been able to design that theoretical "weightless room," which would allow prospective space explorers to float around and actually experience all the curious characteristics of life in null-g. The closest they can come is to place an aircraft in a parabolic dive. This gives the passengers in the cargo area as much as a minute of true weightlessness before the plane has to pull up and return to level flight.

You will hear a number of different terms relating to the situation that results when the pull of gravity is nullified. Weightlessness is the descriptive term most often used by the general public. Many working astronauts call it zero-gravity or zero-g. Scientists generally prefer still another term. Because every object aboard the orbiter, and the orbiter itself, exert a tiny amount of mutual gravitational pull whose magnitude depends on their mass, the scientific community tends to use the word microgravity.

The best method of approximating a weightless environment for long periods of time is the Neutral Buoyancy Simulator (NBS). The simulator at the Marshall Space Flight Center, which you will visit and observe, is a huge tank in which the buoyancy of water is used to duplicate the experience of zero-g. NASA constantly conducts studies in the NBS and at the Johnson Space Center's Wet-F pool designed to perfect the techniques that astronauts will use in performing a wide range of tasks in space.

You will perform similar underwater tasks in a large swimming pool during your Space Camp training. Possible assignments you might be called upon to accomplish include a simulated satellite service mission or working with several team members to build a large structure similar to the "building block" framework of a space station.

But even months of training on the best possible simulators is no substitute for the actual experience of zero-g. The fine art of moving smoothly and efficiently in a world without grav-

Kevin Richardson playfully tries to imitate the space station orbit's weightlessness as he descends from the space station's upper (living) deck to confer with Kelly Harrington, already working in the lab area.

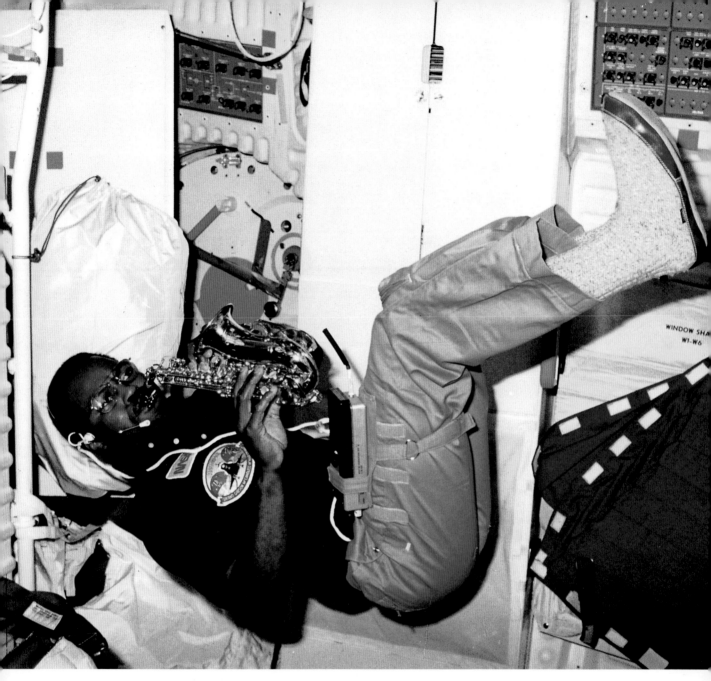

An avid jazz saxophone player, astronaut Ronald McNair takes time out to enjoy the weightlessness of space during mission 41-B.

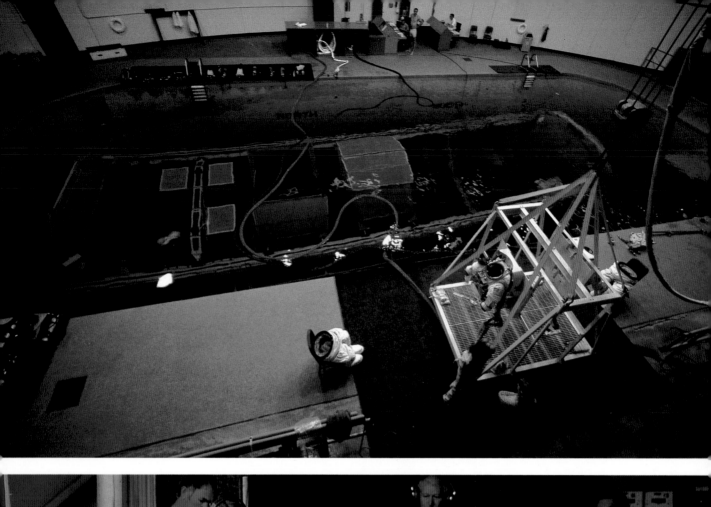

ity must ultimately be perfected in space.

In space, Newton's Third Law will tend to dominate your every waking moment. You will have to be constantly aware of that equal and opposite *reaction* that is the inescapable counterpart to every *action* you perform.

As just one example, if you want to turn a nut with a wrench on Earth, the process is extremely simple (unless, of course, the nut is jammed). You fit your tool to the nut and apply twisting pressure. That is your *action*. Because of gravity's pull, the *reaction* of the nut resisting the force you are applying is transferred through your body to your feet and then to the ground you are standing on.

In weightlessness, this transfer does not take place because there is no gravitational force to lock your feet firmly to the surface. Therefore, when you twist that wrench, it is quite likely that you will twirl around in the air while the nut remains placidly unmoved, right where it started.

You will also have to develop a whole new set of reflexes so that you can glide effortlessly from one work station to the other, instead of launching yourself across the cabin like some new form of unguided missile. It must become second nature to you to use the many handholds and foot straps that are provided to help keep you in place and avoid colliding with things in the cabin or its surfaces as Newton's Third Law predicts you will.

The Physiology of Zero-G

The human body has been conditioned by millions of years of evolution on Earth. In the terminology of the space engineer, all of our "systems" have been designed for this environment, and for no other. Our rigid skeleton supports the heavy weight of our flesh and organs. The incredible strength of our heart muscle is needed to pump blood to our extremities, against the pull of gravity.

In space, all of these forces that we have been built to overcome disappear. So it is hardly surprising that the sudden imposition of weightlessness will have a number of significant effects on your body. None of them appear to be serious or permanent, but you will have to take several specific steps to control them until your body can adjust.

The first condition you will notice is caused by the redistribution of fluids in your body and in the bodies of your fellow space travelers. Everyone's face will appear flushed and a bit puffy, and your sinuses may feel congested. Your body will behave as though there had been a sudden increase in your total supply of blood. It will try to dump these excess fluids by an increase in perspiration and the excretion of urine. Your body weight will drop, and you will lose larger than normal amounts of sodium, potassium and other electrolytes until your body stops trying to compensate for these apparent changes.

Particularly in your first hours of weightlessness, you also might experience the temporary malady that is popularly known as space sickness, and professionally termed Space Adaptation Syndrome. Almost half of all space travelers experience this disorder. Its symptoms include the kind of lethargy that is normally associated with the flu, sometimes coupled with vomiting. Oddly, the vomiting is not preceded by a feeling of nausea.

Physicians first thought this illness was essentially similar to seasickness, which is caused primarily by a disturbance of the motion-sensing organs in the canals of the inner ear. Later studies suggest that the cause may be as much perceptual as it is physical, rooted in a refusal of the eye and the brain to accept the sudden, startling disappearance of up, down and all the other clearcut indicators of earthly equilibrium.

A time-release motion-sickness medication applied to your skin just before launch helps take care of the physical aspects of the problem. Ultimately, usually after a few hours of experience with weightlessness, the marvelous capacity of

top: At Houston's JSC, the WET-F pool holds a model of the shuttle's payload bay. An astronaut will don the EMU upper and lower torso to practice his EVA in the weightlessness of water.

left: Trainees observe astronaut Sherwood (Woody) Spring as he leaves MSFC's NBS pool after a space structures engineering test.

the human mind to adapt to new experiences will overcome your perception problems, and you will have gained your space legs.

> The term sea legs refers to the inner ear's capability to accommodate to an ocean vessel's constant pitching and rolling. Therefore, the phenomenon really has nothing to do with the legs. The term space legs, however, really does describe a phenomenon that affects the lower limbs. Because of a combination of fluid redistribution and lack of exercise, astronauts who spend exceptionally long periods of time in weightlessness have found that their legs, and particularly their calves, grew much thinner. The loss of size was so pronounced that some space voyagers took to calling this phenomenon bird legs.

Because very little physical effort is needed to live in a weightless environment, your space voyage can have some further unfortunate side effects. Your muscles can begin to atrophy—particularly the muscles of the heart and legs—and a steady loss of calcium will begin to cause deterioration of your bones. These conditions sound alarming, and they could be serious if they are ignored. However, the pioneering work of earlier astronauts, particularly the three Skylab teams, have taught us how to control the physical difficulties of space travel.

Research has shown that exercise can help to reduce or totally eliminate the effects of these physical changes. For this reason, your orbiter is equipped with an exercise treadmill, which you are encouraged to use as frequently as possible. Adjustable elastic cords hold you onto the treadmill, allowing you to run in place.

On a normal shuttle mission, which is relatively short, fifteen minutes of exercise a day should be enough to overcome the debilitating effects of weightlessness. On longer missions, daily exercise of thirty minutes or more might be required.

Once you have mastered the peculiar sensation of weightlessness and learned to adapt to its properties, you'll be ready to begin your training for the daily routine of life in space.

previous overleaf and above: After watching astronaut Woody Spring build space structures at NASA's pool, campers enter the weightless environment of water and discover it's harder than they thought to build a structure while floating . . . but not impossible.

below: Jason Cardier returns from the Spacelab into the space station's living quarters. Kelly Harrington emerges from the personal hygiene station and shower area, past the galley.

4.
Living in Space

Daily Routine On Board the Shuttle

Space is an inhospitable environment, infinitely more foreign and hostile to man than the icy cold of the Antarctic. To live in space, therefore, you must control every aspect of your environment totally. The temperature, the food and water supply, even the air you breathe must be maintained artificially, imitating as nearly as possible conditions on Earth. As you have seen, the one condition that cannot be duplicated in space is the effect of the Earth's gravitational pull. Eating, sleeping and working in a weightless environment pose special problems. As you begin your training to perform everyday activities in space, you'll soon find that the designers of your shuttle have found solutions to make life on board relatively comfortable.

Suiting Up

Your crew compartment has a controlled atmosphere that allows you to perform your tasks on board in comfortable, loose sport clothes. On the flight deck, astronauts wear the one-piece blue-cotton flight suit. Most specialists work on board

the shuttle in regulation blue-cotton trousers or shorts and a navy blue short-sleeve knit shirt. A matching blue waist-length jacket completes the outfit. The flight suit's exterior is covered with versatile pockets that close with zippers or Velcro for securing small items. These work clothes are designed for safety and convenience. They have all been treated with a fire-proofing chemical.

The compact nature of the shuttle requires crew members to limit the personal items they bring on board to regulation clothing and accessories. You'll be allowed one set of normal underwear per day, one pair of 1-g footwear per flight and one pair of in-flight footwear, one jacket per flight, one pair of trousers for each seven days of flight and one spare per flight, one shirt for each three days, and one pair of gloves per flight. The small personal items that you may take along include felt-tip and pressurized pens, mechanical pencils, sunglasses, a Swiss Army knife, a pair of surgical scissors and two watches.

When you work outside the spacecraft, you'll need to wear a space suit that is really a "personal spacecraft" designed to protect you from the alien and deadly environment of space. Space is hostile to the unprotected human because of the absence of atmospheric pressure and oxygen to sustain life. In addition, without the filtering effects of the Earth's atmosphere, tem-

left: Astronaut Jerry Ross dons an EMU space suit and snaps his glove into the ring lock. He is about to enter the Neutral Buoyancy Simulator for an EVA training session building space structures.

above: Kelly Harrington in her LEH (Launch and Entry Helmet) in front of Space Camp's shuttle Columbia.

peratures can range from extreme highs of 250° F. to as low as −250° F.

At altitudes above 40,000 feet, the air is so thin and the amount of oxygen so minuscule that conventional pressure oxygen masks are no longer adequate. Space suits must be worn at these altitudes to contain oxygen for breathing and to maintain a pressure around the body so that gases in the blood do not form dangerous bubbles.

> *It sounds astonishing, but space can actually make your blood boil. Air pressure determines the boiling point of a liquid. At sea level, the boiling point of water is 212° F. In the thin air at about 15,000 feet, water will boil at 98.6° F. —the temperature of your body. At 63,000 feet, your blood also would boil at this relatively low temperature.*

Space suits are pressurized to 3.5 pounds per square inch—equivalent to about 34,500 feet in altitude. But you actually have more oxygen to breathe than you do on Earth because the suit is filled with 100 percent oxygen instead of the 20 percent oxygen mixture in Earth's atmosphere.

The space suits used on missions from Mercury through Apollo provided effective protection for the astronaut, but they had certain design flaws. Each garment was custom-fitted for an individual astronaut. In some, more than seventy different measurements were required to ensure a proper fit. This was both a time-consuming and costly process. In addition, space suits were stiff and unwieldy. Even simple motions were fatiguing.

For the Space Shuttle astronauts, a new, improved suit has been developed. Your shuttle space suit is lighter, more durable and flexible and allows more freedom of movement than previous suits.

The shuttle space suit is manufactured in small, medium and large sizes and can be worn by men and women. Two suits are provided on each flight—one for the pilot and one for the ranking mission specialist. The suit, which is worn only outside the shuttle, is modular with many interchangeable parts. Since torso, pants,

top left: A level II trainee tries on her flight coveralls, called IVAs (IntraVehicular Assembly clothing). These are an almost exact replica of those worn by astronauts, with lots of pockets and Velcro for attaching small items.

right: Michael Keenberg struggles into an Apollo-era training suit with the assistance of Chistian Haak of Germany. It's difficult because the suits are heavy with layers of insulation that protect astronauts from the moon's extreme temperatures.

left: ESA Payload Specialist Ernst Messerschmid of Germany snaps down the lid of his pressurized LEH.

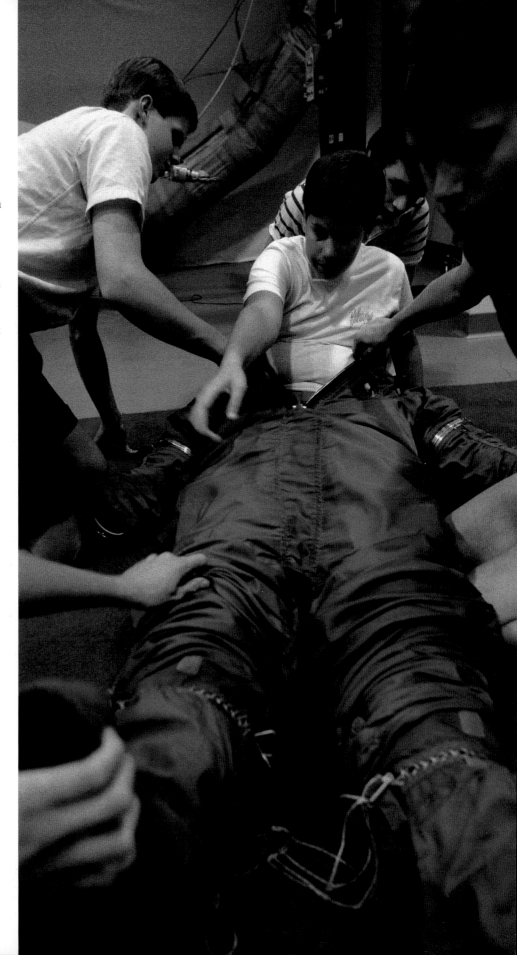

below: Dacia Jessick looks up apprehensively as her space helmet is lowered into place for the first time.

above: Kari Farnham gets used to the feeling of being enclosed in the EVA suit, which is in effect a mini-capsule.

arms and gloves come in different sizes, they can be assembled for each mission in the proper combination to suit the individual astronauts. This modular feature means the space suit can be reused on more than one mission. Each suit has a fifteen-year life expectancy.

The new shuttle suit is called an Extravehicular Mobility Unit. The EMU consists of three main parts: liner, pressure vessel and primary life-support system. Supplemental components include a drink bag, communications set, helmet and visor assembly.

The suit liner—the liquid cooling and vent garment—is similar in appearance to long underwear. The nylon stretch fabric is laced with small plastic tubes. Cool water is circulated around the body through these plastic tubes to control body temperature.

After you have put on this under layer, you are ready to put on the pressure vessel. The outer shell of this multilayered garment is what we see in photographs and normally call the space suit. One interior layer contains the pressure. The others are alternating layers of aluminized Mylar plastic and unwoven Dacron that insulate the suit from the extreme temperatures of outer space. The top layer of tough Ortho fabric serves as an abrasion and tear-resistant cover as well as the primary micrometeoroid shield.

The pressure vessel's principal function is to contain oxygen under pressure to provide the astronaut with a livable atmosphere. One of the major challenges in designing the shuttle space suit has been to make the pressure vessel flexible. With inside pressure, the vessel inflates like a balloon and becomes stiff. Tucks stitched in the shoulder, elbow, wrist, knee and ankle areas allow the joints to retain a flexed shape without strenuous muscle exertion.

The final component of the shuttle suit is the Primary Life Support System. The PLSS is a two-part system comprised of a backpack unit and a control and display unit on the suit chest. The backpack portion of the PLSS supplies oxygen for breathing, suit pressurization and ventilation. It detoxifies the suit's atmosphere, cleansing it of carbon dioxide and other contaminants. And it cools and circulates the water used in the liquid cooling and vent garment to maintain body temperature.

Your space suit is a totally self-contained apparatus that provides approximately a seven-hour oxygen and electric supply, depending on the extent of your exertion. This allows fifteen minutes to check out the suit, six hours for extravehicular activity, fifteen minutes to take off your suit and thirty minutes for reserve. There is also an extra half-hour emergency supply of oxygen in the secondary oxygen pack.

Because it is relatively heavy and complex, attachment of the PLSS on Apollo space suits was an arduous process. It has been simplified in the shuttle suit by placing a fiberglass shell inside the upper torso of the pressure vessel. This shell is called the Hard Upper Torso. The PLSS is permanently mounted to the HUT and all necessary connections are made through the suit's upper layers.

On the front of the HUT you'll find a control unit and a display panel. This is actually a computer on a microchip circuit that automatically supplies start-up instructions, checks out the suit's major functions and warns the wearer of malfunctions.

The space suit requires a separate system for handling containment of body wastes. Actually two different systems have been designed for urine excretion—one for men and one for women. Due to the relatively short durations of space-suit activity, fecal containment is considered unnecessary.

The final items you'll need for your space suit to be complete are the helmet and visor assembly. The helmet is a rigid, one-piece hemisphere made of ultraviolet polycarbonate plastic. When the helmet is in place, the upper torso and helmet portions of the suit ventilation system are automatically aligned. On top of the helmet is a visor assembly that provides impact, light and thermal protection to the head.

The helmet is placed over a skull cap, called a Snoopy cap. It holds a microphone and earphones that you'll use for communication. Also, before finally donning your helmet, you'll place a small in-suit drinking bag filled with 950 ml. of water inside the neck area of the HUT. A drink tube with a suction-actuated valve permits occasional refreshment during your EVA.

To suit up, you will enter an air lock between the flight deck and the cargo bay. First you'll put on the appropriate urine collection system and the liquid cooling and vent garment. You'll find the upper torso of the pressure vessel and the PLSS mounted to one of the air-lock walls. You'll pull on the pants and then "dive" into the upper torso. The pants and upper torso are joined at the waist by a metal ring connector. After the life-support system is actuated and all connections are made, the communications cap, helmet, visor assembly and gloves are attached. You'll find that you can complete the entire procedure without assistance and be ready for work in just a few minutes.

The Manned Maneuvering Unit (MMU) is a one-man propulsion backpack that snaps onto the back of the space suit's portable life-support system. The MMU allows the crew member to work outside the orbiter without a tether and to move as far as 300 feet from the orbiter. It is designed to provide EVA support for as much as six hours at a time. You'll use it to complete repairs outside the shuttle and to travel from the orbiter to other orbiting spacecraft.

The MMU weighs 255 pounds and is propelled by nitrogen gas fed to twenty-four thruster jets. Two pressurized nitrogen tanks can be refilled from the orbiter's on-board supply. All systems on the MMU are "dual redundant"—if one system fails, the second system can take over completely.

You'll control your MMU with two hand controllers on the ends of the MMU's armrests. It is equipped with attach points for cameras, tool kits, lights and power tools.

Food Preparation

If you had been among the original astronauts, you would have found your meals in space extremely unappetizing. During the early space flights, meals were restricted to items that could be puréed and placed in metal squeeze-tubes or compressed into bite-sized tablets. The Gemini

JSC Suit Technician Jean Alexander fits astronaut Story Musgrave for his LEH and EMU upper torso. She will add the personal touches he desires, like the flag on the table.

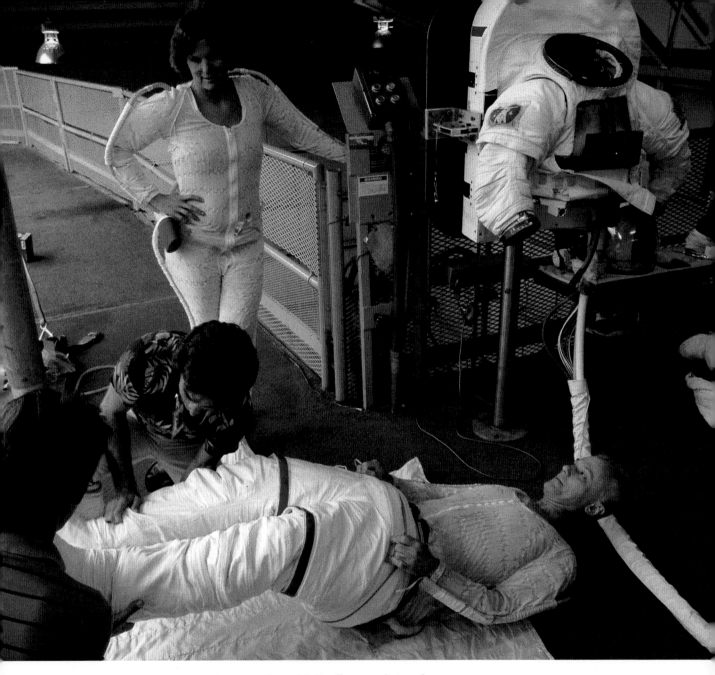

Astronaut Bruce McCandless crawls into the lower torso of his EMU training suit. The upper torso is on the rack behind him. Astronaut Kathy Sullivan wears her liquid-cooled garment waiting to don her EMU before a space telescope prelaunch EVA simulation.

astronauts were introduced to freeze-dried foods that could be rehydrated and the Apollo astronauts were able to add some canned foods and fresh bread to the menu. The Apollo team also used "spoon-bowl" packaging for the first time, which meant they could eat with a spoon instead of squeezing the food through a slit in the package. Not only did they find they were able to use a spoon successfully, but they found the spoon didn't even have to be held right side up.

Skylab had a freezer, so astronauts aboard the orbiting laboratory could enjoy filet mignon, lobster newburg and even ice cream. Space-flight cuisine has come a long way. You'll be glad to know your meals on board the Space Shuttle have been designed to be both nutritious and appetizing.

There are two food-preparation systems on board the shuttle—a portable system that can be stowed in a number of mid-deck lockers and a multipurpose galley and personal-hygiene station. The space requirements of a particular mission determine which system will be appropriate. When the galley station is used, it is located in the mid-deck near the entry hatch.

Food on the shuttle is categorized as menu food or pantry food. The menu food supply contains food for three recommended meals per day per crew member. The pantry food supply contains snack items and a two-day contingency food supply. A standard menu of three recommended meals plus between-meal snacks and beverages provides an average 2,100 calories per day.

Meals come in a variety of different forms and packaging. For example, thermostabilized foods are heat-processed and come in cans or laminated foil pouches. Freeze-dried foods are dehydrated and need to be reconstituted with water. Foods and beverages such as scrambled eggs, chicken and noodles, coffee and lemonade come in this form in plastic containers. Irradiated foods are preserved by exposure to ionizing radiation. Bread, rolls and meats that are preserved in this manner come in plastic pouches. Some foods are preserved by controlling the moisture, such as dried apricots or dried peaches. These interme-diate moisture foods come bite-size in plastic pouches. And, finally, certain foods, such as nuts and cookies, can be transported to space in their natural form. These ready-to-eat foods are also sealed in plastic pouches.

The water dispenser provides the shuttle crew with ambient and chilled water for food and beverage rehydration, as well as for hygiene. Because liquids in space will not slide down the edge of a glass, all beverages must be drunk through straws.

Food trays on the shuttle provide an individual dining surface for each crew member. The trays are color-coded for each person on board. The tray has a variety of restraint devices to hold food and accessories. These devices include indentations, spring clips, magnetic strips and Velcro.

A portable heating unit, called the food warmer, can warm food for four crew members within one hour. The food is heated by thermal conduction using a hot plate enclosed in an aluminum suitcase. You'll only use the food warmer on missions where the galley is not installed.

Crew members take turns "cooking." When it's your turn, you'll find that you can prepare a meal for a crew of seven in about twenty minutes. After the meal, empty food containers are stowed in one of the wet-trash compartments. You'll clean your tray and utensils with germicidal wet wipes so they can be reused.

Sleeping on the Shuttle

Your sleeping accommodations on the shuttle have been designed for comfort and privacy. Several different sleeping provisions are available on the shuttle. Rigid sleep stations may be used on some flights. The four rigid sleep stations (three horizontal and one vertical) contain a sleeping bag, a personal stowage area, a light and ventilation ducts. These stations are more than 6 feet long and 30 inches wide. Each sleeping bag is attached to a padded board. In weightlessness, the sleeping bag holds the astronaut against the hard board with just enough pressure to create the illusion of sleeping on a comfortable mattress.

If the rigid sleep stations are not flown on your

above: A NASA suit technician conducts a structural and leak check on an EMU suit before it's used for a training session.

right: Astronaut Bruce McCandless explains his EMU suit to a Space Camp trainee visiting MSFC during a break in his space telescope training session. Astronauts will meet with trainees *if* their schedules permit. The lower torso is not attached during the break so it will not pull and strain Bruce's shoulders with its weight. The whole suit weighs 250 pounds on Earth.

previous overleaf: During habitability training at JSC's 1-G trainer, payload and mission specialists (*left to right:* Dr. John Konrad, Dr. Stephen Cunningham of Hughes Communications, Dr. Ernst Messerschmid and Dr. Reinhold Furrer of ESA) learn to operate the galley by making dinner using space-rated food prepared in individual portions.

left: Kelly Harrington holds a tray of astronaut food in the mid-deck. The tray restrains food and utensils.

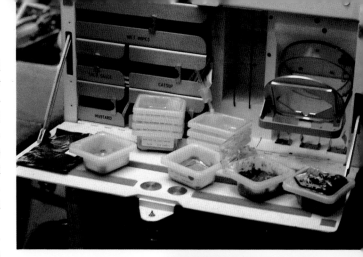

mission, a personal cotton sleeping bag is issued for each of the four crew members. Clamps allow these sleeping bags to be attached to the mid-deck locker face in either a horizontal or vertical configuration. Two adjustable, elastic body restraints hold the upper and lower portions of the body. A zipper on each side of the bag allows it to be attached to a support pad for better rigidity. A cotton-padded pillow can be attached to a head restraint with Velcro strips.

If your mission crew has more than four members, Apollo sleeping bags are provided for the additional people. The Apollo sleeping bag has four adjustable straps with clamps that connect to any two lockers. These sleeping bags are stowed in a mid-deck locker.

above: Food preparation station of the galley onboard the shuttle.

You will also be issued a sleep kit, which stows in your clothing locker for launch and return. Each kit contains eye covers and ear plugs. When the shuttle crew exceeds four, crew members ordinarily sleep in shifts, so there is likely to be continuous activity on board while you're trying to sleep. Eight hours are set aside for sleep, with forty-five minutes to prepare for bed and forty-five minutes for personal hygiene upon awakening. Most astronauts find, however, that they need only about six hours sleep because they don't use a lot of physical energy in weightlessness. Astronauts have found sleep in space to be restful, but tests show that sleeping in space is not quite the same as sleep here on Earth. For one, tests on Skylab astronauts showed that there is a change in the length of time spent at various levels of sleep. Also, some astronauts are bothered by a peculiar effect called head nod. During sleep the head develops a nodding motion, which is thought to be the result of blood pulsing through the large arteries in the back of the neck.

right: The first major component donned for the EMU suit is the Liquid Cooling and Vent Garment.

Some of the space-rated Personal Hygiene Kit items.

Personal Hygiene and Waste Management

Personal hygiene presents a sizable problem for spaceflight. Male-female crew combinations living in close quarters require considerable thought in designing functional systems. Compared to previous systems, the facilities on board the Space Shuttle are quite civilized. Most of the personal-hygiene functions are performed on the orbiter mid-deck.

right: A webbed line, with tether clips on each end, hangs on the EMU suit.

above: Gloves worn with the EMU shuttle suit during EVA.

left: The pressurized LEH and Anti-Gravity suit are worn only during launch and entry.

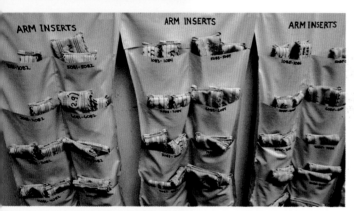

above: These inserts are assembled inside the modular EMU shuttle EVA suit to make a proper fit.

left: In a NASA suit room components of two EMU suits are laid out.

Although Skylab had a shower, it worked poorly and crews preferred the standard towel baths of earlier spaceflights. The shuttle crews, therefore, have returned to towel baths. Each astronaut is issued one towel and two washcloths per day. Rubber restraints with a Velcro base allow the crew members to hang their towels and washcloths on the waste-management door or the mid-deck walls.

Shaving can be done with electric razor or blade. A Personal Hygiene Kit (PHK) is furnished to each crew member to provide for brushing teeth, shaving, hair and nail care. In addition, a Female Preference Kit (FPK) is provided to female crew members with articles essential to female hygiene and grooming.

An integrated Waste Collection System is located next to the side hatch. The multifunctional WCS collects, processes and stores solid and liquid wastes. The orbiter's commode resembles a standard toilet, operating on the centrifuge principle. Located in a closet in the mid-deck, it is used by both men and women.

While all these new systems will take some getting used to, you will find life in the orbiter surprisingly comfortable. The orbiter's combined living volume of only 790 cubic feet becomes relatively roomy in space when the ceilings and walls are every bit as habitable as the floor. Since there is no up or down in your weightless home, most astronauts prefer to keep their bodies oriented toward the orbiter's own up-down configuration, as this makes it easier to read dials or to rummage through storage drawers. The one big problem in this situation is that there is no place to set down an object. Nothing has any weight to hold it down, so shelves, tables and even floors are useless. Every object that needs to stay in position must be somehow hooked, clamped or held in place with a Velcro or adhesive strip. Even crew members themselves often have to be anchored to accomplish some stationary task. Now that you've encountered some of the basics of life on the orbiter and learned to deal with zero-gravity, it's time to begin your actual mission training.

Astronaut Sherwood "Woody" Spring, right, talks to a Space Camp trainee who is in his own EMU space suit and is working an accurately detailed MMU mock-up. Spring was training at MSFC, building EASE space structures, and stopped by Space Camp to share his experiences.

5.
Mission Training

Astronaut Selection and Preparation

Astronauts undergo years of hard work, education and training before they begin to prepare for a specific mission. At Space Camp you'll participate in two separate missions, giving you a chance to be part of a shuttle crew, and to learn about mission control operations. While your Space Camp training will focus primarily on the tasks you will actually perform on your mission, you'll want to learn as much as possible about many other aspects of astronaut training, assignments and mission preparation.

Astronaut Selection

When NASA began selecting the first American astronauts in 1959, the candidates had to be qualified jet pilots who had graduated from test-pilot school and had a college degree in engineering. They were also required to have fifteen hundred hours of flying time. More than five hundred men qualified. After military and medical records were examined, psychological, physical and

left: On a visit to Space Camp during a break in their space structure EVA training, astronauts Jerry Ross, left, and Woody Spring pass on the finer points of structure construction. The trainee's structure is in the foreground.

above: Astronaut Bruce McCandless, a mission specialist, evaluates procedures he will use on his MMU test mission, 41-B. The T-PAD attachment on the MMU arm allows the astronaut to "capture" or rendezvous with the malfunctioning Solar Maximum satellite.

technical tests conducted and reconducted, NASA announced its selection of the first seven astronauts. Three were Air Force captains: L. Gordon Cooper, Jr., Virgil I. "Gus" Grissom and Donald K. "Deke" Slayton; two were Navy lieutenant commanders: Walter M. Schirra, Jr., and Alan B. Shepard, Jr.; M. Scott Carpenter was a Navy lieutenant and John H. Glenn, Jr., was a Marine lieutenant colonel.

Three years after that first selection, NASA issued another call for astronaut trainees for the upcoming Gemini and Apollo programs. The selection criteria still emphasized experience in flying high-performance aircraft and quality of education. At this time the program was opened to qualified civilians. In September 1962, nine new trainees were announced. By October 1963, when fourteen additional astronauts were selected, NASA's primary emphasis had shifted from flight experience toward superior academic qualifications. And a year later applications were solicited on the basis of educational background alone. These were the scientist-astronauts, so-called because each of the applicants who met the minimum requirements had a doctorate or equivalent experience in natural sciences, medicine or engineering.

In consultation with the National Academy of Sciences in Washington, D.C., NASA selected six of these astronauts in June 1965. Although the call for volunteers did not specify flight experience, two of these applicants were qualified jet pilots and did not need the year of basic flight training given the others. From this point until today, NASA astronauts have fallen into two basic categories—pilot-astronauts and scientist-astronauts.

The first group of astronauts selected after the initiation of the shuttle program were chosen in January 1978. This group included twenty mission specialists and fifteen pilots. Six of the thirty-five were women—the first to join the astronaut corps—and four were members of minorities. In August 1979 NASA announced plans to begin accepting applications for Space Shuttle astronauts on an annual basis.

Pilot-Astronauts

NASA pilot-astronauts serve in both commander and pilot positions on shuttle missions. To qualify as a pilot candidate, you'll need a bachelor's degree in engineering, biological or physical science or mathematics. The quality of your academic preparation is extremely important, and an advanced degree or equivalent experience is also desirable. To meet the minimum qualifications, you'll also need at least one thousand hours of pilot-in-command time in high-performance jet aircraft. Test flight experience is a plus. As a pilot applicant, you'll be required to pass a NASA Class I spaceflight physical (similar to military and civilian flight physicals), which includes the following standards:

Distant visual acuity: 20/50 or better uncorrected; corrected 20/20 in each eye.
Hearing loss not to exceed:

Frequency (Hz)	*500*	*1000*	*2000*
Loss (db)	30	25	25 per ISO (1964 standard)

Blood pressure: Preponderant systolic not to exceed 140; diastolic not to exceed 90mm Hg, measured in sitting position.
Applicant height between 64 and 76 inches.

Orbiter Commander

If you're assigned to the position of commander

above left: A Space Camp commander at work in the flight desk during his mission.

above right: McCandless docks and retrieves the Solar Max satellite during an EVA simulation.

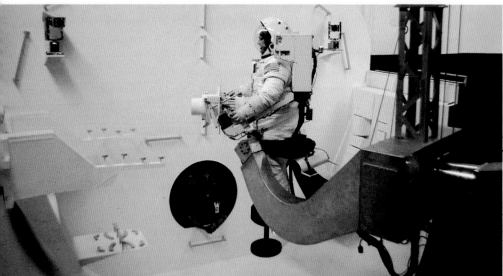

left: McCandless developing flight techniques for the MMU in a Space Operations Shuttle Simulator. Computer software is the key to the almost exact simulation here on Earth of MMU reactions in space.

or pilot for your Space Camp mission, you will be responsible for flying the orbiter. The commander occupies the left front seat of the cockpit and is the final authority on all matters concerning the flight. The commander is ultimately responsible for every operation inside the shuttle during the mission. In an emergency situation, his decisions are final. His primary job is that of controlling the shuttle during launch and reentry. The job of commander is similar to that of the captain of a commercial airliner.

Orbiter Pilot

The commander and the pilot share flight duties. Together they maneuver the orbiter in flight. At Space Camp you will be in command whenever the commander is not at the controls. The pilot takes charge should anything happen to the commander during the mission. He is also capable of landing the orbiter safely. The pilot's job is similar to the copilot on a commercial airplane.

Payload Specialists

Payload specialists are scientists and engineers, usually employed by a private company or foreign countries to perform scientific and technical investigations on board the shuttle, or to operate specialized equipment while in Earth orbit. As a payload specialist, you will have received the majority of your training from the organization that has developed the payload to which you are assigned. However, you will be required to complete approximately 150 hours of training at the Johnson Space Center. This training, not unlike the program at Space Camp, will familiarize you with the STS vehicle and payload support equipment, crew operations, housekeeping and emergency procedures. NASA retains the final selection authority, even of payload specialists, to ensure those chosen can function as part of the flight crew.

Mission Specialist Astronauts

The mission specialist is a scientist-astronaut who performs experiments while in orbit.

To qualify as a NASA mission specialist candidate, you'll be required to hold a bachelor's degree in engineering, biological or physical science or mathematics. Your degree must be sup-

plemented by at least three years of related experience. An advanced degree in your scientific discipline is desirable and can be substituted for the experience requirement. For example, a master's degree is equivalent to one year of experience and a Ph.D. equals three years.

Mission specialist astronauts must be able to pass a NASA Class II spaceflight physical, which includes the following standards:

Distant visual acuity: 20/100 uncorrected; correctable to 20/20 each eye.

Hearing loss not to exceed:

Frequency (Hz)	500	1000	2000
Loss (db)			
Better ear	30	25	25
Worse ear	35	30	30 per ISO (1964 standard)

Blood pressure: Preponderant systolic not to exceed 140, nor diastolic to exceed 90mm Hg, measured in sitting position.

Applicant height must be between 60 and 76 inches.

If you are assigned to be a mission specialist at Space Camp, you will perform EVAs to repair a malfunctioning satellite and to work on building a large space structure. You will also work with the payload specialists to perform experiments in Spacelab.

Flight Assignments

Once you are assigned to a flight crew, your schedule will be very busy. Crews are assigned to specific shuttle flights well in advance of the launch date. Because Space Shuttle flights are intended to occur at relatively frequent intervals, several crews will be training at the same time.

Each crew member receives cross-training, so that at least one other person can handle the most critical duties of each associate. For the early operational test flights, a backup crew went through identical training. In this way, an ill or injured person could be replaced before the flight with-

---

right: **Deep in concentration, astronaut William Fisher uses hand controls on the MMU simulator to move in the x, y and z axes, (pitch, yaw and roll).**

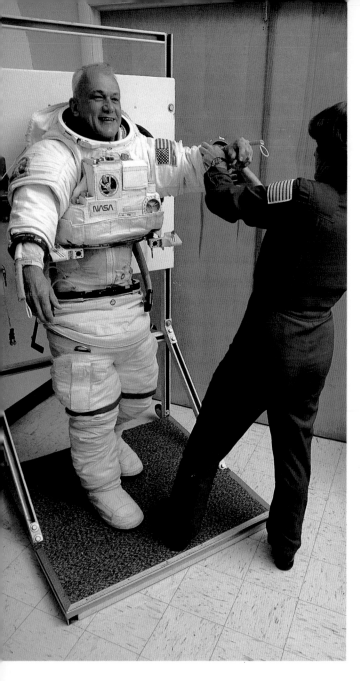

Astronaut Mission Specialist Kathryn Sullivan assists Bruce McCandless donning an EMU suit prior to an MMU space operations simulation.

out compromising the mission.

The tempo also picks up for the Space Camp astronauts when they receive their mission assignments. They begin working with various simulators to learn the individual tasks they will be expected to perform and to perfect their timing so they can complete their job within the allotted mission sequence.

The simulators used by NASA astronauts, like those you will use at Space Camp, provide extremely realistic working conditions. To familiarize you with zero-g and prepare you for an EVA assignment, five simulators are utilized.

The *One-sixth-Gravity Moon Walk* simulator shows you what it would be like if your weight were reduced to its equivalent on the moon.

The *Zero-Gravity* simulator goes one step further, to give you an approximation of total weightlessness. You sit in a chair that is held at the ends of two long, pivoting arms. When your Earth weight is precisely counterbalanced, the slightest effort will cause you to float far above the ground.

You will spend a good deal of time training with the *Five Degrees of Freedom* simulator (5DF). As you attempt to perform mission tasks, it will spin, tumble and move in various directions, just as you would do in a weightless condition.

The *Manned Maneuvering Unit* simulator (MMU) is a full scale mock-up of the real apparatus. When mated with Space Camp's *Remote Manipulator System* (RMS arm), the unit gives the student much of the same independent control over his own position in space as an astronaut on EVA.

The *Multiaxis Trainer* was used in the early days of spaceflight and is still used in some aspects of training for current space missions. It is designed to help an astronaut learn to adjust to a state of disorientation in space.

The orbiter simulator used at Space Camp is extremely realistic. The spacecraft interiors are duplicated and the instruments are programmed to give the same readings they would in flight. Even out-the-window views of Earth, stars, payloads and the landing runway are projected onto screens where the spacecraft windows would be.

By the time astronauts go on their actual mission, most have the sensation that they have made the flight many times before because the training has been so realistic.

During a typical shuttle flight, there are generally two to eight people aboard the orbiter. On the ground, however, there are literally hundreds of directors and support personnel covering every aspect of the mission.

The Space Camp mission is based on twenty positions—ten flight positions and ten ground positions. Each trainee gets a chance to train and experience two positions, one on the ground and one in the flight crew. Your Space Camp ground assignments vary somewhat from an actual mission control situation because you're working with many fewer people. Nonetheless, you'll get a very realistic idea of how trained flight directors on the ground work with the astronauts to ensure a successful mission.

Launch/Landing Director

At Space Camp, for example, if you are assigned to be the launch/landing director, you will be in charge of the countdown up to launch and must make sure that "all systems are go" for a safe and on-time lift-off. If there are problems, the launch director can stop the countdown with a "hold" up until T − 30 seconds. You can terminate the count or the mission with an abort at any time. When the shuttle returns to Earth, you are in charge of making sure all conditions at the chosen landing site are correct for landing and that all support equipment is in place.

Flight Director

The flight director is responsible for the operation of the orbiter and shuttle system from ignition to touchdown. You will give the shuttle crew the "okay" for all planned and unplanned maneuvers and for the beginning and termination of all EVAs. During the launch, you will keep the shuttle crew informed about their progress and performance. The flight director is the person in control of the mission from the ground. You make the final decision if there appear to be problems or abnormalities in the mission. If there are problems during the launch, you can call for a Return To Launch Site (RTLS), Trans Atlantic

Astronaut Kathryn Sullivan uses hand controls to fire the 24 nitrogen jet thrusters on an MMU simulator allowing her to maneuver in space during an EVA. Lights indicate the thrusters have been activated.

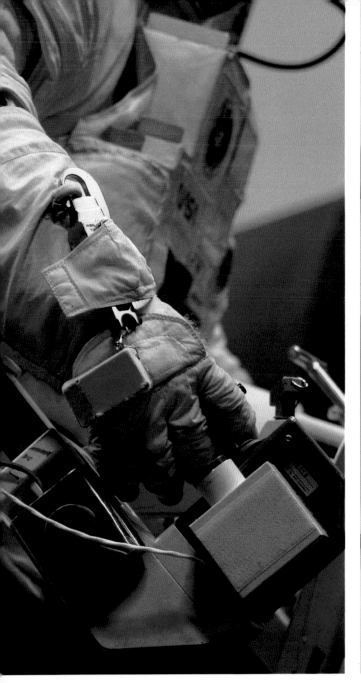

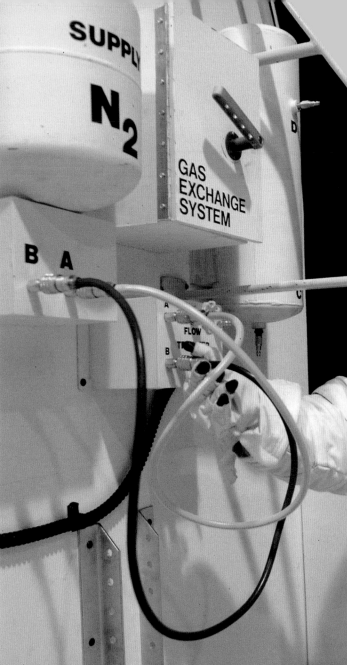

Close-up of an astronaut using the hand
controls of the MMU simulator. The
hand controls are the "steering wheels"
of the MMU and precise movements are
necessary, so astronauts log as many
hours of simulation time as possible.

Landing (TAL), an Abort Once Around (AOA) or an Abort To Orbit (ATO).

Mission Director

The mission director at Space Camp is in charge of the overall operation of the Spacelab mission. If this is your assignment, you will approve any activity in Spacelab before it begins. You will need to coordinate with the flight director to make sure all activities stay as close as possible to the defined time-line.

Commercial Payload Representative (CPR)

This person in mission control is not a government employee, but an independent civilian employed by the contractors who have payloads on board the shuttle. In this role, for example, you will monitor satellites. If a satellite appears to be grossly off course, you have the ability to change its course. The CPR verifies that satellites launched are working properly and offers advice if there are any problems with commercial payloads on the flight.

Weather/Tracking Officer

The weather/tracking officer is crucial in all launch and landing activities. In this capacity, you must verify that all conditions (wind, visibility and cloud cover) are acceptable for a safe launch and landing. As the tracking officer, you will keep track of the orbiter's position and any Losses Of Signal (LOS) that occur. You'll also be expected to verify independent tracking from ground-based stations of satellites launched from the shuttle.

Communications Director

This member of mission control is responsible for making sure that all communication lines with the orbiter are functioning normally and that links with the Tracking Data Relay Satellite System (TDRSS) satellites are working normally. You'll also perform periodic audio checks with the orbiter. At Space Camp the communications director also performs many of the duties of the Cap-Com (Capsule Communicator) in talking with the shuttle crew before and after periods of LOS. Finally, you will also be the person who provides commentary about the flight, translating

In the aft section of the shuttle's payload bay at Space Camp, Kelly Harrington makes the necessary repairs on the gas exchange system during an EVA.

many of NASA's terms into language that the public can understand.

Orbiter Systems Director (OSD)

The Orbiter Systems Director is responsible from countdown and launch to the final landing for the mechanical operation of the shuttle. In this assignment, you will monitor the pressurization of the fuel tanks, as well as the cabin pressure of the orbiter. You'll verify main engine and SRB ignition at launch and supervise problems such as low fuel propellant during the mission.

Principle Investigators

These are scientists who work with the payload specialists during the mission on scientific experiments in the areas of life and biological sciences, physics or materials processing. Very often, they have been working for years on certain experiments before they are performed in space. If you are assigned to this position at Space Camp, you'll keep logs of the tests performed by the payload specialists in the Spacelab and endeavor to make some preliminary judgments about the investigations.

At Space Camp, you and your mission team will participate in a complete premission simulation to familiarize yourselves with the way the full mission activity will be conducted. Your mission simulations will be nearly identical to actual NASA shuttle missions.

Extravehicular Activity Simulation (EVA)

Space Camp trainees participate in three EVA simulations. During the first test mission, you'll perform such basic skills as unstowage, handling of tools and moving objects of large mass. Activities such as these were attempted on NASA missions STS-6 and 41-B. These exercises test the dexterity of the trainee as well as the design of the EVA equipment. One of your first tasks will be to deploy and retrieve the American flag, using the RMS arm. Another task will involve operating hand tools to remove modules from a task board. Also, during this first simulation, you'll be asked to transfer an object of relatively heavy mass (a film canister) from one area to another. To accomplish this task, you will use the 5DF to simulate weightlessness.

previous overleaf: Lee Olyniec uses a laser light transmitted through parallel slits to create a hologram. This investigates the diffraction and interference patterns. NASA uses holograms to study crystal growth in microgravity conditions.

above: His crewmates watch as a trainee turns a light on with a Robotic Arm.

In your second EVA simulation you will construct a large four-sided tetrahedron out of fiberglass beams. One of NASA's hopes for building the Space Station in the next decade is called EASE: Experimental Assembly of Structures in EVA. This project involves the assembly of these pyramid modules to assess astronaut capabilities and to evaluate the design for a large space structure. This entire activity hinges on how well you and your team work together. You'll have to learn to operate the MMU to perform this activity.

One of the primary uses of the shuttle, from its earliest conception to the present, is to use the orbiter as a satellite repair service. The orbiter and her crew can capture a failing satellite and perform any necessary adjustments, including repair, refueling or returning it to Earth. Your third EVA simulation at Space Camp involves retrieving a satellite, replacing a failed communications module and refueling the satellite before releasing it. Teamwork is critical to your success, just as it was for the astronauts on the eleventh flight of the Space Shuttle. In April of 1984, using their MMUs, a team of mission specialists successfully captured and repaired "Solar Max" . . . the ailing Solar Maximum Mission Observatory Satellite.

Payloads

An important part of your Space Camp training involves learning to handle the various kinds of payloads that the shuttle might carry into space. Shuttle payloads are classed as either attached—such as Spacelab—or free-flying—such as a satellite.

If you are either a mission specialist or a payload specialist, you will be performing a number of investigations in Spacelab during this mission. For example, you'll do a glucose test to determine the effect of space travel on blood-sugar levels; you'll investigate space sickness and you'll conduct laser experiments. You'll also perform experiments analyzing the growth of crystals in microgravity.

You'll be advised before launch if your mission is carrying a Getaway Special (GAS) payload. These are Small Self-Contained Payloads (SSCP) sent to space by individuals or compa-

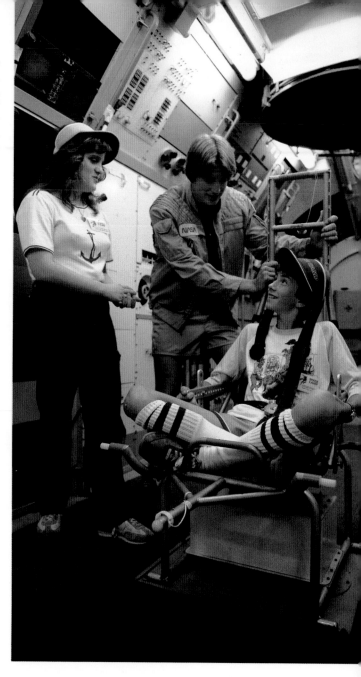

These Space Camp trainees were fortunate to have a NASA student trainee show them the inside of the Spacelab training mock-up at MSFC.

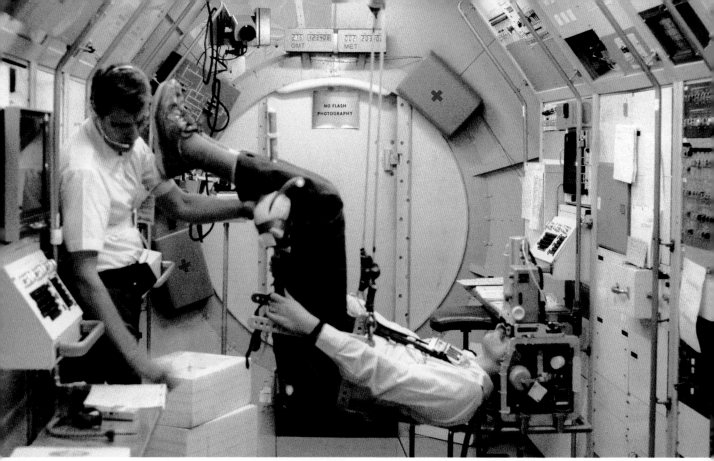

above: In the Spacelab module mock-up, Dr. Byron Lichtenberg, left, monitors Dr. Michael Lampton in the rotating Body Restraint System. Lampton wears an eye measurement and infrared helmet, which measures eye movement. This life science experiment measures motion in micro-gravity to learn how the body will work with the different types of motion in space.

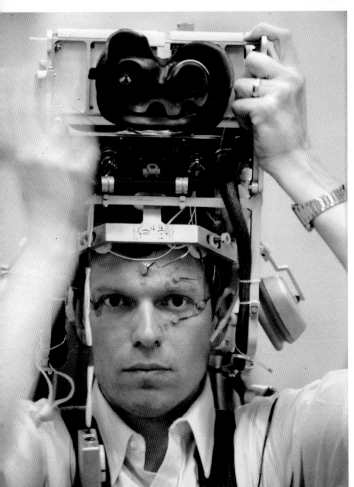

left: During a timelined mission practice, Lichtenberg prepares himself as a test subject for the life sciences experiment "Effects of Rectilinear Acceleration in Space." The sensors monitor movement, probing the interactions between man's equilibratory/vestibular system and his brain, with the goal of understanding the causes of Space Adaption Syndrome.

nies other than NASA and the large aerospace firms. The Getaway Special concept has been extremely popular. By the time Columbia made her first flight in April 1981, more than three hundred had been sold. Successful GAS payloads have even been sent to space by high school and college students. These payloads are sent to space in small, cylindrical containers, mounted either to the side of the shuttle cargo bay or bridging the cargo bay. NASA can fly as many as twelve Getaway Specials at one time. The GAS container is about the size of a large garbage can (5 cubic feet: 30 inches in diameter and 60 inches high) and can weigh a maximum of 200 pounds. This canister will hold as many as four different experiments and costs $10,000. A canister of the same size but half the weight would cost $5,000. The smallest available canister, which is half the size and weight of the largest, can be purchased for $2,500.

NASA's guidelines attempt to place as few restrictions as possible on these payloads. In addition to the size and weight limitations, the payloads must aid research or development and must require no shuttle services. This means they must have their own power, handling data and environmental controls. An astronaut will turn them on or off from the crew station, but otherwise they must be completely automatic and self-contained. The Getaway Specials are flown on a space-available basis, determined by the weight and volume restrictions on each specific orbiter mission.

Emergency Training

Now that you have an idea of your mission routine and the tasks you will perform on board the shuttle, let's consider the necessary emergency procedures.

Launch Aborts

An abort means the mission must be stopped immediately because of an emergency condition. There are two categories of launch aborts—those that occur on the launchpad and those that occur during ascent. A launchpad abort can happen anytime before the solid boosters ignite. Pad aborts require you to exit the orbiter quickly. You will exit through the hatch and get into one of

above: Working at Mission Control requires a lot of concentration, even during mission simulations.

below: NASA's Marshall Space Flight Center's Mission Control Center during a launch. MSFC has responsibility for many functions, such as the SRBs and Spacelab.

left: Project Manager (and Space Camp lecturer) Konrad Dannenberg checks a canister insertion on Project Explorer GetAway Special # 007 before it is given to NASA. The experiment was developed, designed and built by students. This GetAway Special flew on mission 61-C.

Visiting with the trainees after their mission, astronaut Woody Spring shares his first-hand experience in space.

After mission simulation, Space Camp
trainees debrief.

five baskets on slide wires that extend from the service structure to an underground bunker twelve hundred feet away. When you see that all crew members are in a basket, release the brake and slide down the wire. When you reach the landing zone, in about thirty-five seconds, get out of the basket and go to the bunker.

Once the SRBs ignite, you are committed to at least a partial flight. A launch abort occurs if one or two of your orbiter's main engines fail. Several abort options exist. The choice depends on when the failure occurs. Return to Launch Site (RTLS) is used if the main propulsion system malfunctions in the first 4 minutes and 20 seconds of flight. The next abort option is an emergency landing at the Naval Air Station in Rota, Spain. This option applies only to launches from the Kennedy Space Center. The Abort Once Around (AOA) procedure is used when one or two main engines fail after the solid boosters burn out and before an abort to orbit is possible. In this mode you will make a suborbital flight to the emergency landing strip in White Sands, New Mexico —four-fifths of the way eastward around the world from your launch site in Florida. The last launch abort is an Abort To Orbit. The ATO is used if a main engine fails late in the ascent. Slightly longer than usual OMS burns will enable you to reach a lower-than-planned orbit. You'll have to go to an alternate mission plan, but you'll probably be able to complete many of your mission objectives.

In-flight Emergencies

A major equipment malfunction in space may require you to end your mission early. It could even require rescue by another orbiter. Emergencies such as failure of the solid rocket boosters to separate automatically or failure of the main engines to throttle automatically are relatively easily handled by manual control. Other emergencies are more serious. For on-board fires, there are three built-in remote-control fire extinguishers and four portable ones. Smoke detectors are located in all three electronic equipment areas in the mid-deck and in the inhabited areas of the crew compartment. If a fire or smoke is detected, a light on the flight deck shows the fire's location, and an alarm sounds. If you hear an alarm, you will don a Portable Oxygen System (POS) and employ the appropriate fire extinguisher.

Problems involving the cabin's atmosphere can be grave. If the problem involves the oxygen life-support system, use the emergency supply. If you can't repair the system, a rescue mission will be necessary. You and your crew will have to transfer to the rescue craft. There are only two space suits on board. Nonspace-suited crew members will use the personal rescue enclosures or rescue ball. Wearing your POS, you'll climb into the ball and another crew member will zip it shut. The space-suited astronauts will transfer you to the rescue ship during a space walk. You will also use the rescue ball if toxic gas contaminates the cabin. After all crew members are in a space suit or rescue ball, the astronauts in suits will depressurize the entire cabin, venting the air along with the toxic gas. When the cabin has been repressurized, everyone can remove their rescue ball or space suit.

Medical Emergencies

The Shuttle Orbiter Medical System (SOMS) is a three-part medical kit that is stored in the mid-deck. It will enable you to handle any simple illnesses or injuries that occur during flight. The kit also has equipment that allows you to stabilize severely injured crew members until you can return to Earth.

Entry and Landing Emergencies

Normally both OMS engines fire during your deorbit maneuver. However, if one fails to fire, the other can slow you enough for your return. In the unlikely event that both OMS engines fail, you'll use your maneuvering rockets for descent. If you are forced to land in a remote area, there is a survival kit on board containing enough equipment to sustain a seven-person crew for forty-eight-hours.

Your Space Camp training is now complete. You are ready for your Space Shuttle mission.

Konrad Dannenberg, a member of Wernher von Braun's rocket team and former Deputy Director of Mission Payload Planning Development at MSFC, explains his involvement with the development of this Saturn V rocket to Space Camp trainees from around the world.

6.
Your Mission in Space

The Moment You Have Worked For

It's an hour after dawn at Florida's Cape Canaveral. The sun has burned off an early-morning haze, and only a few widely scattered clouds mar the perfection of the blue sky.

The moment every astronaut works for, trains for, waits for has finally arrived. Poised on its tail like a giant bird clasping its two solid rocket boosters and its massive external fuel tank, the Space Shuttle orbiter is ready for lift-off.

It's also Mission Day at Space Camp. You get up at 6:45 A.M., dress quickly and spend half an hour in vigorous astronaut conditioning. A quick shower is followed by an even quicker breakfast.

After arriving at Pad 39A at the Kennedy Space Center, the astronaut takes the long elevator ride to Level 195 of the service tower. A stroll along a steel catwalk brings him to the white room that adjoins the one-meter-wide hatch leading to the orbiter's flight deck.

Technicians help each crew member into his

or her assigned seat . . . first the commander, then the pilot, then the mission and payload specialists. The process is a bit awkward, because the seats are now lying on their backs.

The Space Camp mission crew don their Launch and Entry Helmets (LEHs) and check that all straps are tight and securely buckled.

The astronaut's senses remind him that his space vehicle is slowly coming alive. He hears groaning, hissing and rumbling noises as the liquid hydrogen and oxygen in the external tank bubble and fume. He removes a pack of Velcro-backed cards from his flight-data file, attaches them to the instrument panel and begins final preflight checks.

At Space Camp, you do exactly the same thing. Communications with Launch Control and Mission Control are verified. Your Abort Advisory System (AAS) is checked. The side hatch is closed and you begin a cabin-leak check. The demanding list of precisely defined verifications gains a momentum of its own, moving you and your crew members toward the moment of launch.

Let's pick up the countdown on a typical Space Camp mission.

T −4:25   *Orbiter Systems Director*
Roger Shuttle, we confirm positive auxiliary power start, and I'm switching you to internal power.

---

left: "5 . . . 4 . . . 3 . . . 2 . . . 1 . . . Wow! We have Solid Rocket Ignition and Lift-off of the shuttle Columbia from Space Camp! This is neat!" crows the Launch Director at Mission Control.

above: "At plus five seconds, the shuttle has cleared the tower. You can start that roll, I mean, we have roll maneuver start," continues the L.D. Turning to the Flight Director he adds, "We did it! All right!"

Commander
Roger, we're on internal.

T −3:45 *Flight Director*
Shuttle control surfaces are in position and ready for launch and engine gimbal checks are underway.

Upon receiving the Launch Director's instructions, you lower the visor on your helmet and turn the volume control on your communications up full. It's going to get very noisy in just a little while.

T −1:00 *Commander*
External fuel tank now at flight pressure.

T −0:40 *Orbiter Systems Director*
Roger Shuttle, you are GO for launch. We have auto sequencer start.

T −0:31 *Commander*
Roger auto sequencer.

Launch Control has now shifted to your on-board systems. Your shuttle is fully independent.

T −0:15 *Communications Officer*
T minus 15. Counting down. 10, 9, 8 . . .

Like the breaking of a dam, you hear the sound of thousands of gallons of water suddenly flooding into a pit at the base of the launchpad. When the searing flames of the solid rocket boosters reach it, the water will instantly turn to billows of steam, serving as a buffer against the roar and vibration of the engines—which otherwise would seriously damage the orbiter's flight structures and payload.

T −0:06 *Launch Director*
Main engine start.

Massive valves in the external fuel tank open, letting supercold liquid oxygen and hydrogen flow to the three main engines. The liquids mix, are ignited and begin pouring out a thrust of 1.12 million pounds.

Commander
Roger, all three engines.

You hear the immense roar as the main engines attain power and feel the orbiter lurch suddenly toward the external tank.

0:00:00 *Launch Director*
Solid rocket ignition and lift-off!

Two searing bursts of flame surge into the hollow core of the solid rocket boosters, igniting the powdered aluminum propellant. In less than a second a white-hot core of flame bursts from each booster, generating a combined thrust of more than 5 million pounds.

The noise on the flight deck, already intense, becomes thunderous—an awesome roar interspersed with a crackling sound like fat in a superheated pan.

Eight explosive charges release the bolts that hold the vehicle assembly on the pad.

0:00:04 *Pilot*
Engines steady at 104 percent.

The service tower, visible out of your left side window, seems to vanish almost instantly. You feel yourself pressed back into your chair as the launch vehicle breaks the shackles that bind it to the Earth and seeks its natural element in space.

0:00:11 *Flight Director*
We have roll maneuver start.

Your shuttle is rotated so that you are now flying in a "heads down" attitude.

0:00:30 *Commander*
Roll maneuver complete. Course bearing 90 degrees.

0:00:35 *Weather/Tracking Officer*
Range report: Velocity 950 feet per second.

0:00:40 *Flight Director*
Shuttle, you're nearing Mach 1 and are GO for throttle down.

0:00:45 *Pilot*
Engines now at 65 percent, as programmed.

0:01:06 *Flight Director*
Shuttle, you're at Max-Q and GO for throttle up.

above: Commander:
"Roger. Go for throttle up."

left: STS-1, April 12, 1981.
Astronaut John Young is
commander of America's
first Space Shuttle,
Columbia, on its maiden
space flight. "The dream is
alive again."

above: "Don't screw up that GetAway Special deployment, Dacia, people have already paid for it!" The camera keeps Mission Control abreast of their activities, but not of all their commentary.

right: Payload Specialist Gaby Glatzer gets to work in the Spacelab, measuring the critical angle of incidence that exists when light rays approach the surface of liquid. "When light rays exceed this angle, no light will emerge from the material. Amazing."

Communications Officer
"Max-Q" means that the shuttle is experiencing maximum aerodynamic pressure. The engines will be returned to full power.

0:01:45　*Communications Officer*
We're approximately 15 seconds away from SRB separation.

You slide forward in your seat as the orbiter decelerates. The solid fuel rocket boosters have burned themselves out. The sky, now a deep ebony black, is briefly illuminated by a vibrant flash of light. The SRBs have separated and are being thrust away from the orbiter and the external tank by small rocket motors. Now that the SRBs' deafening roar has ended, the sound of your main engines seems, by comparison, merely a friendly background hum.

0:02:30　*Weather/Tracking Officer*
Range Report: Velocity 6,100 feet per second, altitude 35 nautical miles, downrange 25 nautical miles.

0:02:50　*Flight Director*
Shuttle, you have two-engine TAL capability.

　　　　　Pilot
Roger, two-engine TAL.

　　　　　Communications Officer
Two-engine TAL means that the shuttle now has enough velocity to land across the Atlantic at Dakar, Senegal International Airport, if a single engine failed.

0:07:05　*Weather/Tracking Officer*
Range Report: Velocity 17,000 feet per second, altitude 63 nautical miles, downrange 250 nautical miles.

0:07:30　*Flight Director*
Shuttle, you are GO for throttle down.

0:07:45　*Commander*
Roger, GO for throttle down 65 percent.

0:07:50　*Communications Officer*
The three main engines are now

throttling back to 65 percent in preparation for main engine cutoff.

0:08:10　*Commander*
MECO, Houston, we have main engine cutoff.

Again you slide forward in your seat as the thrust of the main engines stops. The bolts connecting the orbiter to the empty tank explode automatically. Reaction control motors in your spacecraft ignite, gently nudging you away from the tank as it begins its long plunge toward the Indian Ocean.

A two-and-a-half-minute burn of your OMS engines adds another 130 mph to your speed . . . just enough to place the shuttle in an elliptical orbit. As you reach your farthest orbital distance from the Earth, a second OMS burn will place the shuttle in a near-perfect circular orbit.

You have arrived in space. Now it's time to get to work.

As soon as their Space Shuttle simulator successfully achieves stable orbit, Space Camp's mission and payload specialists begin a wide variety of assigned tasks. Scientific investigators briskly enter the air lock and tunnel leading to a working model of Spacelab.

One Spacelab investigator is soon pumping hard on an exercyle. Periodically, another investigator will take a blood sample to measure the effect of this exertion on glucose levels.

Another Space Camp scientist is whirling on a swivel chair as part of an experiment to determine the effects of disorientation on reaction time—a vital matter for astronauts who must constantly function at peak efficiency in space.

Nearby, a payload specialist exposes different fluids to light to gather data on their capacities to retain solar energy.

Student scientists also work with lasers and fiber optics, study holograms, develop techniques to grow microcrystals and examine the behavior of a colony of ants under "microgravity" conditions.

Outside the orbiter, the schedule of work is equally intense. A fully space-suited EVA team is preparing a satellite for deployment. A second group, using the 5DF and MMU simulators are

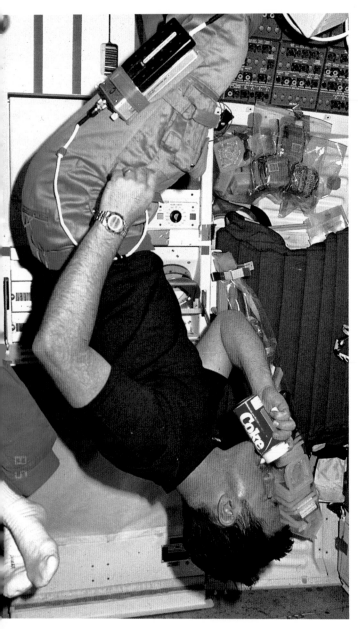

top left: Astronaut Anthony England finds
that Coca-Cola is the real thing on mission
51-F. A special dispenser was developed to
keep the fizz inside the can, not floating all
over the cabin.

top right: The OAST Solar Array
Deployment Structure test article was
deployed to its 70 percent extension level
against an Earth background. 41-D Mission
Specialist Kathy Sullivan commented
"Now that's a pretty sight." This array folds
down into a 7-inch box!

constructing a component for a complex space structure.

The time approaches to head for home. You and your fellow crew members shut down experiments and restow equipment. The massive cargo-bay doors are closed.

L−1:15:00 *Pilot*

Houston, deorbit preparations are complete, and we're standing by to turn the orbiter around for a deorbit burn.

Flight Director

Roger Shuttle, you may turn the orbiter around in preparation for deorbit burn.

Communications Officer

The Commander will now place the shuttle in a tail-first attitude, so that the OMS engines will fire in the proper direction to slow the shuttle down for reentry.

Your orbiter is passing over the night side of the Earth. If you could see through the darkness beneath your spacecraft, you would note that you are passing over the East African coast. Halfway around the globe at Edwards Air Force Base, California, your designated landing site, it is already full daylight. You feel a gentle nudge of deceleration as the OMS engines fire. By the time the burn is complete two minutes later, the orbiter has been slowed by only 200 mph. But trimming even that tiny fraction of speed from its pace of more than 17,000 mph will be enough to send it on its way back to Earth.

L−0:41:00 *Commander*

Houston, we're beginning atmospheric reentry.

Your spacecraft has lost slightly more than half of its orbital altitude. Because its nose is pointing upward at an angle of about 35 degrees, the tile-coated belly of the vehicle is the first to touch the widely scattered molecules that mark the upper boundary of Earth's atmosphere. The orbiter's tremendous speed, close to Mach 25, strongly compresses the steadily thickening wall of air. Friction builds up, and with it, heat. Protective

above: Mission Specialist Joseph Allen is a human test subject for Dr. Norman Thagard onboard Columbia during mission STS-5.

left: Astronaut James D. (Ox) van Hoften was entrusted with caring for 3,000 bees by high-school senior Dan Poskevich of Waverly, Tennessee. Dan was a participant in the Shuttle Student Involvement Program. His idea was to have a space bee colony and an Earth bee colony, and to monitor their activities simultaneously.

above: Mission Specialist Rob Reider to Mission Control: "All GetAway Special functions executed nominally, lookin' good up here."

right: Mission Specialist Carol Heron to the Flight Director: "Houston, the communications satellite deployed . . . looks like a good deploy . . . yes sir, it's slowly moving away from the shuttle."

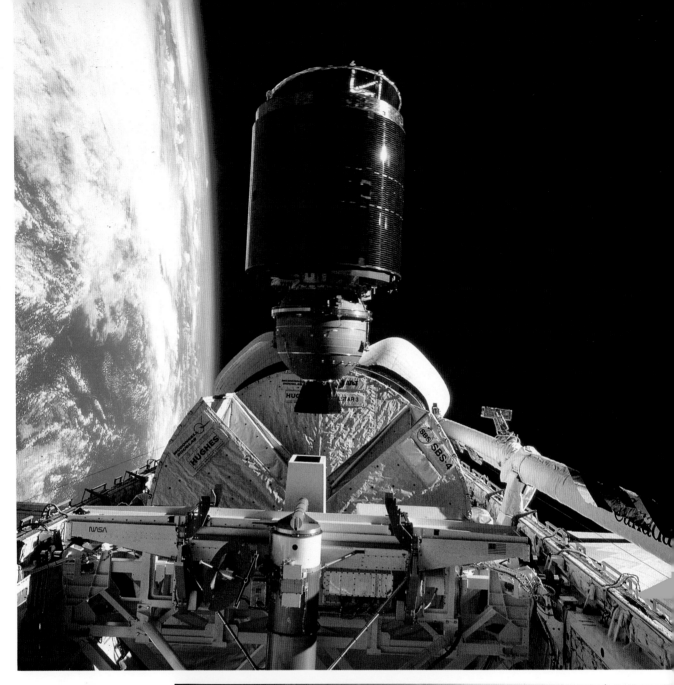

above: The SBS-4 communications satellite, moments after deployment by the Discovery shuttle crew, lifts above the payload bay. Rockets on the satellite fire and send it toward its orbital destination during mission 41-D.

right: Mission Specialist Michael Lounge, left, and pilot Dick Covey, right, viewed from the Discovery payload bay during William Fisher's EVA during mission 51-I.

previous overleaf: Bird's-eye view of a mission in progress at Space Camp: counselor Greg Dowdell, left, operates the MMU on the Remote Manipulator Arm as trainees complete EVA activities on the Spacelab pallet, rear, and on the Space Telescope, right foreground. The flight deck and Spacelab are on the left.

above: "This is hard to do floating all over the place . . . hold it . . . I think I've got it now," grumbled a trainee. Working with a power tool modified for zero-gravity use, she struggled to remove a module from a task board during her EVA.

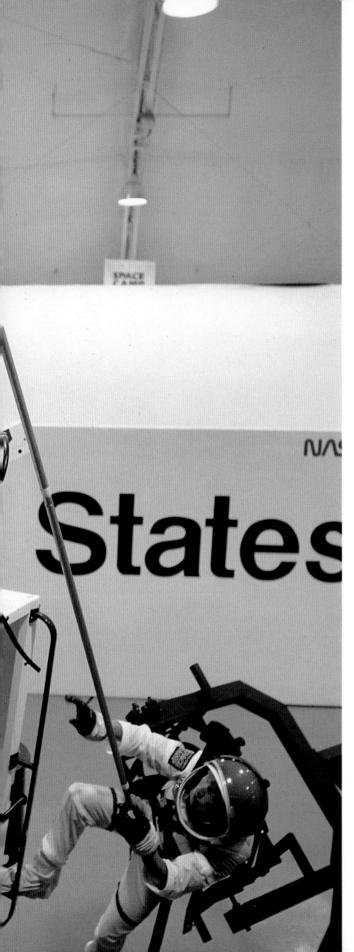

tiles in the most strongly affected areas, such as the nose and the leading edges of the wings, reach 2,500° F. The craft's complex cocoon of protective tiles dissipates the heat as it is generated so that, on the flight deck, you do not feel even the slightest discomfort.

For the first time since lift-off, you begin to feel the effects of gravity. It quickly passes through Earth Normal, to 1.5 g—not really much, but after days of weightlessness, you feel as if you are being crushed. You can hear the air rushing past the spacecraft's body. At first, it was just a whisper, but it soon builds to a shriek. The tiles begin to glow as they ward off the increasing temperature. You see a faint reddish glow through the cockpit windows. Soon this glow covers the entire spacecraft, enclosing your vehicle in a blanket of incandescence. The glow brightens . . . turns from red to orange to pink, and then to a searing white.

The intense heat of reentry boils electrons from the surrounding air, wrapping the orbiter in a veil of ionized vapor that will cut off all communications with the ground. This condition generally lasts about twelve minutes.

As you pass over the Pacific Ocean on your way to Edwards, you are still traveling at many times the speed of sound. To dump this speed, you must perform a series of sweeping S-shaped turns, called roll reversals. You tilt your vehicle 90 degrees onto one side, and then roll it back in a similar tilt in the other direction. Your elevons begin to bite solidly on the increasingly dense air. Your orbiter has assumed its role as a glider, able to be steered with the control surfaces on its wings and tail.

Your spacecraft is now in a phase called Terminal Area Energy Management (TAEM). Simply stated, this means that the vehicle must be flown in such a way that it will arrive at its intended destination at precisely the right speed and altitude to assure a perfect touchdown. Because the orbiter lacks power, there is no chance to fly around and try again.

left: "Catch this or it's lost in space," says Erik Christensen to John Spangler, using the MMU to change a part on the Spacelab Experiments Pallet during their EVA.

above: Astronauts Story Musgrave, center, and Don Peterson perform the first experimental EVA of the shuttle era during the 51st, 52nd and 53rd orbits of STS-6 at 17,500 m.p.h. and 177 miles above Earth.

right: Following the successful recovery of two wayward satellites, astronaut Joe Allen photographs fellow mission specialist Dale Gardner. Reflected in Gardner's helmet are Allen and the orbiter Discovery during mission 51-A.

far right: Mission Specialist Dale Gardner inserts the stinger into the wayward Westar satellite's exhaust nozzle, capturing it. Gardner, using the MMU to move, then used the circular ring to pull the satellite back to the payload bay.

The Heading Alignment Cylinder (HAC) is, in effect, an imaginary circle three-and-a-half miles in diameter resting in front of and just to one side of the runway. On your final approach, you will fly a partial circle around this HAC, until you are correctly aligned with the runway entry point.

L − 0:05:30 *Landing Officer*
Shuttle, you're approaching the HAC. Stand by to turn when ready.

Commander
Roger Houston, ready to initiate turn.

You are on a 22-degree glide slope, heading straight for the runway. For every four-and-a-half feet of forward motion, you are losing one foot of altitude. That's a little bit better glide characteristic than a falling stone—but not much. To correct this, so that you will touch the runway reasonably gently, you must flare the orbiter's nose upward to a much shallower angle of 1.5 degrees.

L − 0:00:30 *Pilot*
Landing gear armed.

Landing Officer
Confirmed.

L − 0:00:15 *Pilot*
Gear down and locked.

L − 0:00:10 *Commander*
Full flare.

The main landing gear scuffs the surface of the runway, kicking up puffs of smoke. Then the nose wheel touches down. The speed brake and wheel brakes are on full. Like a tired tour bus, your orbiter lumbers down the runway, gradually rolling to a stop.

The voice of your best friend at Space Camp, dripping with sarcasm, fills your earphones. "Congratulations, turkey, I thought you'd never make it."

Welcome home!

above: "I'm just hanging around doing some work," a suspended Jay Pate says of his "weightless" activities in the Spacelab, while John Lunde tests the changes in cardiopulmonary rates during exercise in a zero-gravity environment.

right: Payload Specialist Ulf Merbold is the test subject monitoring the effects of vestibular disorientation and motion to probe the causes of Space Adaptation Sickness onboard the Spacelab.

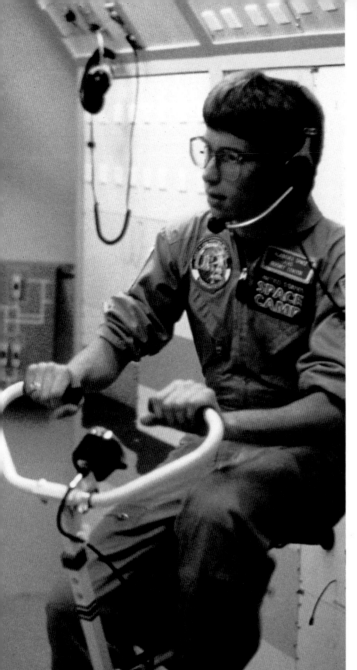

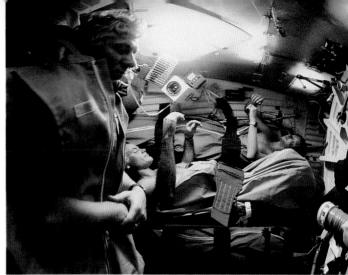

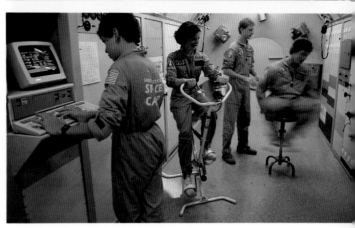

top right: Sleeping in weightlessness.

above: In Space Camp's Spacelab the crew is busy conducting life science experiments, too. Wendy Gale researches the effects of exercise on Vital Lung Capacity (VLC) while John Spangler tests the effects of circular motion on the reaction time of Craig Fleishman.

top left: Mission Control yells, "Touchdown, main gear! Plenty of room left, fantastic job!" After the shuttle's fiery reentry, it makes the transition from a steering rocket to a powerless glider, and lands at a speed of 215 m.p.h.—twice that of a commercial jet landing.

above: "Roger, Columbia, proceed as planned, the landing convoy is in position along the runway. We can see your approach now. Go for it!"

left: The pilot acknowledges approaching blackout: "Roger, Houston, we can see the tiles heating up, we'll see you on the other side of the hill." Flight controllers in the Mission Control Room at JSC monitor the orbiter at all times except for the brief blackout during reentry.

7.
The Next Step

The Space Telescope and Space Station

Man has forever dreamed of flight. Yet not even a hundred years have passed since Wilbur and Orville Wright first flew their primitive airplane over the sand dunes at Kitty Hawk, North Carolina. As recently as thirty years ago, space travel and habitation still belonged solely to the realm of science fiction. Today, man has become a frequent traveler to space, and we are reminded daily through modern technology of the advantages that we have derived from space exploration. The communications satellites that relay our phone calls and bring us instant television images of far-distant events, the tremendous advances in solar-energy production, the miniaturization of electronic components that makes digital watches, calculators and home computers smaller and increasingly affordable, materials development and medical progress represent only a fraction of the benefits that have resulted directly and indirectly from space technology.

Already we are able to envision new directions in space exploration. We have mastered the first rudiments of space travel and overcome the environmental obstacles, so that we can spend extended periods away from Earth. Now we can concentrate on learning more about our universe from an extraterrestrial vantage point. We will shift our emphasis from exploratory missions to operational missions. Having learned to adapt to the demands of space, we are now ready to take advantage of its unique properties and bend them to our needs. We are about to make the transition from short-duration missions as occasional visitors to major projects that will make us year-round residents and workers in space.

The space transportation system will carry many of us to space in the coming decades. By the year 2000, journalists, physicians, instrument makers, geologists, meteorologists, artists and welders will be among those who accompany traditional astronauts into orbit, participating in a wide array of scientific investigations and commercial activities. Our progress continues at a pace that even science fiction cannot surpass.

The Hubble Space Telescope

When it is launched in 1987, the Hubble Space Telescope will greatly enhance the astronomer's capacity for observation. For more than a century, astronomers have dreamed of viewing the

left: The shuttle interfaces with a space station in orbit over Earth. This configuration of the space station is the way it will probably be built.

above: Steve Poth defies gravity as he negotiates the tunnel that connects the shuttle's flight deck and Spacelab with the space station.

sky through a telescope in space, where vision would not be obscured by the Earth's atmosphere. Today, this dream is a reality. Relatively small telescopes, such as NASA's Ultraviolet Explorer and Orbiting Astronomical Observatory, are already in orbit. But now NASA has designed and built a much larger, more sophisticated instrument called the Edwin P. Hubble Space Telescope, an unmanned optical telescope launched by the Space Shuttle. The Hubble Space Telescope, which is the most powerful telescope ever built, will orbit high above the hazy and turbulent atmosphere, enabling scientists to gaze farther into space than was ever previously possible —perhaps to the outer edges of the universe.

The largest Earth-based telescopes in operation today can see an estimated 2 billion light-years (about 12 billion trillion miles) into space. From its Earth orbit at an altitude of approximately 310 miles with an orbital inclination of 28.5 degrees, the space telescope will be able to see nearly 14 billion light-years. Some scientists believe the universe was formed nearly 14 billion years ago, so the space telescope might provide views of galaxies at the time they were formed.

From Earth, both distance and clarity inhibit our ability to study the stars. All Earth-bound optical devices have distorted vision because the Earth's atmosphere blurs the view and smears the light. The clearer images provided by the space telescope will enable scientists to evaluate the mass, size, shape, age and evolution of the universe more comprehensively. With a telescope in Earth orbit, time-exposure images will be more than ten times sharper than those from the ground. The crisper images of the telescope, combined with the darker sky background, will also permit much fainter objects to be detected.

Space-suited astronauts will be able to service the space telescope in orbit, and to upgrade its equipment and scientific instruments, maintaining it at a state-of-the-art level. The modular design of the telescope will enable astronauts to replace components without affecting the overall system. If major repairs or refurbishment are needed, the shuttle crew will retrieve the space telescope and return it to Earth to be relaunched

above: During an EVA simulation in the
weightless environment of water at MSFC's
NBS, Mission Specialist Bruce McCandless
prepares the space telescope for deployment
in the payload bay mock-up.

left: The Hubble Space Telescope will peer 14 billion years
into the past, unlocking 97 percent of the universe's
history, even possibly seeing the Big Bang! The telescope's
incredible resolution and clarity is possible because its
view into space is not distorted by Earth's atmosphere.

HUBBLE SPACE TELESCOPE
SUPPORT SYSTEMS MODULE DESIGN FEATURES

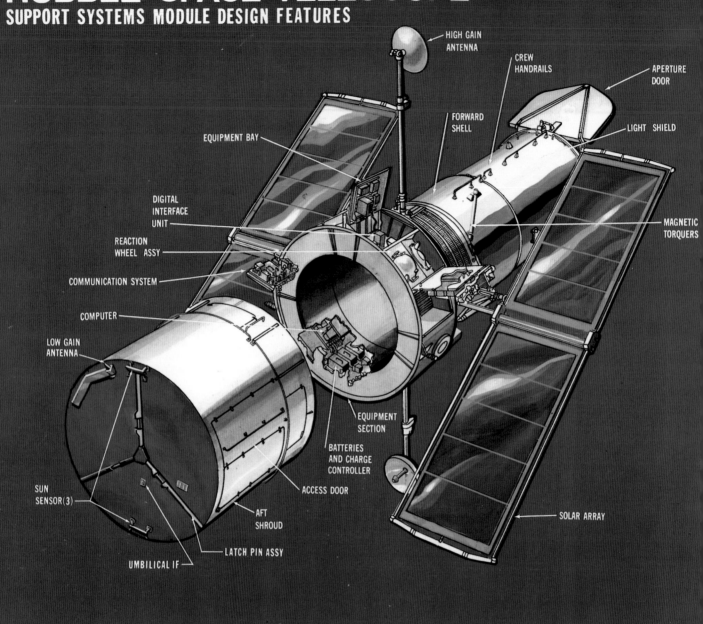

HIGH GAIN ANTENNA

CREW HANDRAILS

APERTURE DOOR

FORWARD SHELL

LIGHT SHIELD

EQUIPMENT BAY

MAGNETIC TORQUERS

DIGITAL INTERFACE UNIT

REACTION WHEEL ASSY

COMMUNICATION SYSTEM

COMPUTER

LOW GAIN ANTENNA

EQUIPMENT SECTION

SUN SENSOR(3)

BATTERIES AND CHARGE CONTROLLER

ACCESS DOOR

AFT SHROUD

SOLAR ARRAY

LATCH PIN ASSY

UMBILICAL IF

right: The space telescope being deployed from the shuttle, and being returned to the payload bay.

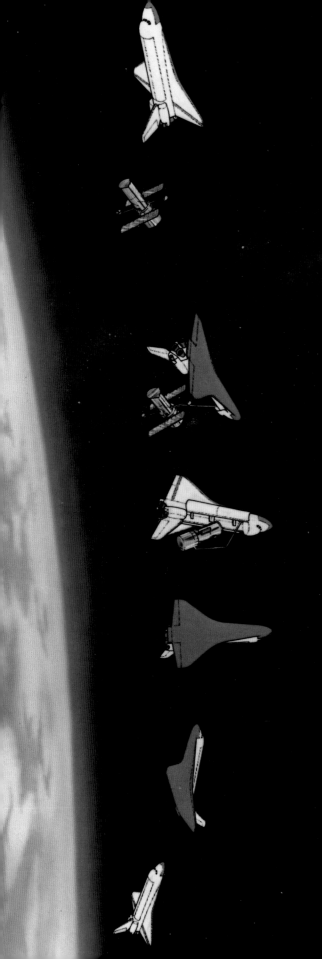

later. The telescope's long-design lifetime will enable it to operate at the forefront of astronomical research for two decades or more.

The Manned Space Station

If the space telescope will allow us to gaze on distant stars, the space station will be a major step toward reaching them.

"We can follow our dream to distant stars, living and working in space for peaceful economic and scientific gain," said President Ronald Reagan in his 1984 State of the Union message. "Tonight, I am directing NASA to develop a permanently manned space station and to do it within a decade."

With those words, the President of the United States set a deadline for Americans to be living and working in space. Once the station goes into operation in the 1990s, Earth's space environment will never be without the presence of Americans.

In this one respect, Space Camp is slightly ahead of NASA, in that it already has a working prototype of a space station. NASA's project is still on the drawing boards. The new space station will be designed and built in the next eight to ten years from sections, or modules, prefabricated on Earth. These will be transported to orbit in the shuttle's cargo bay. There they will be unloaded and assembled by astronauts wearing space suits and propelling themselves with MMUs. Your erection of a large aluminum tetrahedron during your Space Camp training and mission actually simulates the method in which the space station will be constructed.

One module of the space station will be furnished as living quarters for from six to eight people. Additional modules will be outfitted as a combined workshop and laboratory. Atmospheric conditions will be regulated so the crew can work in a shirt-sleeve environment, as they do aboard the shuttle. Other attached modules will carry utilities, such as power-generating machinery, and storage space for equipment. From the beginning, the space station will be designed for evolutionary growth. Additional modules can be added later if larger crews and more equipment are needed. Unmanned scientific plat-

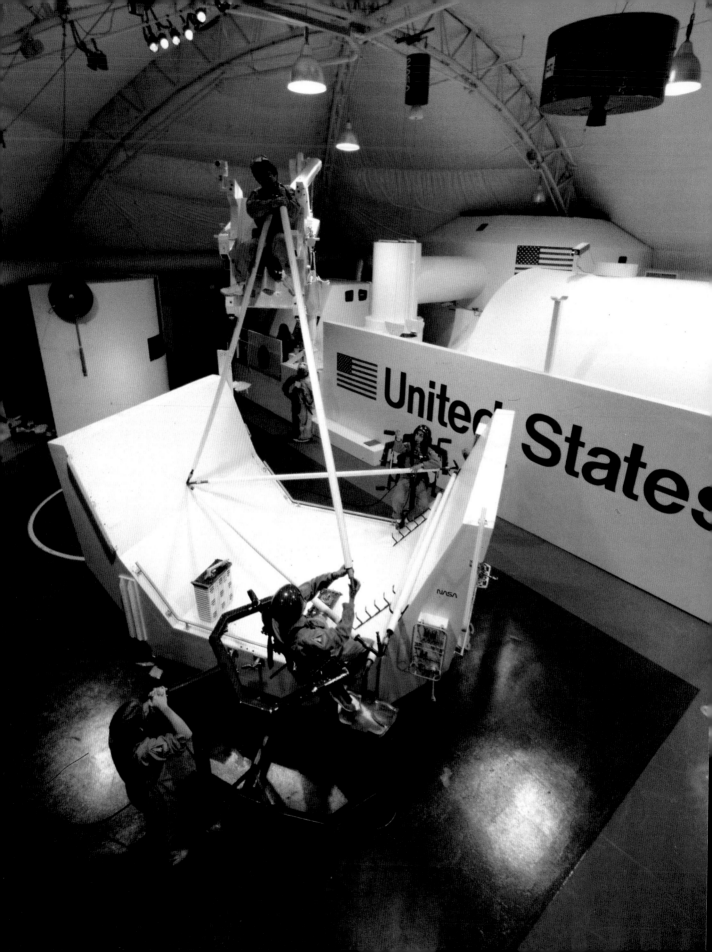

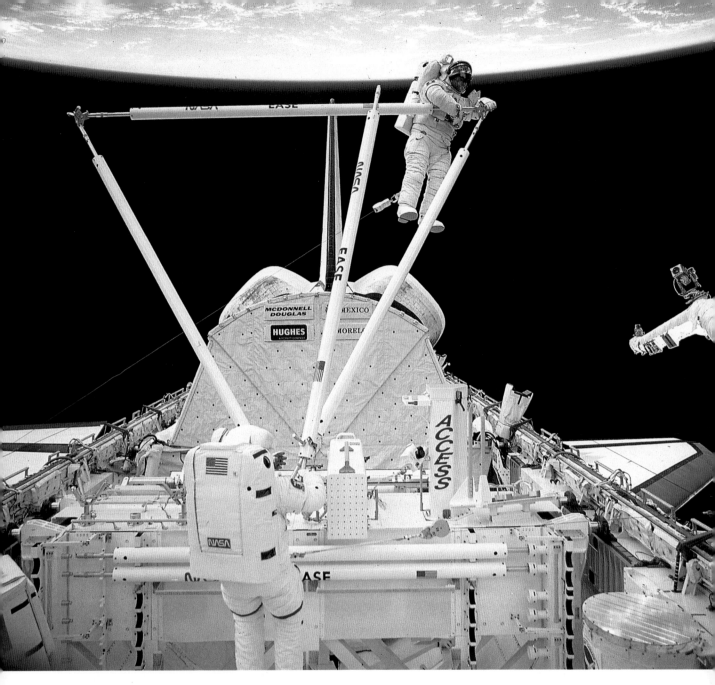

left: During a Space Camp mission, trainees, using flight simulation hardware and mock-ups, build a space structure on a pallet just a few feet away from the Spacelab anchored in the shuttle's payload bay.

above: 61-B mission specialists, Jerry L. Ross, left, and Sherwood Spring begin the building of the Experimental Assembly of Structures in EVA (EASE). They were so well-trained that during their mission they finished faster than expected and had time left to frolic in space's weightlessness.

forms, called pallets, can also be added later. The space station can be self-sufficient for several weeks or even months, although plans call for the shuttle to deliver replacement crews or supplies every few weeks.

Aboard the space station, crews will carry out basic research in medicine, astronomy, space physics and solar studies. Repeated experiments in Apollo, Skylab and shuttle flights have shown that in the microgravity environment materials can be imbued with unique and valuable properties unobtainable on Earth. New medicines, new components for complex electronic equipment and new metal alloys are among the products that look promising for development in space. The space station will provide a regular, reliable, cost-effective access to orbit and a suitable place to carry on the continued research leading to these commercial uses of space.

Trainees at Space Camp already have the opportunity to perform experiments in holography, physics, chemistry and space medicine in their proto-space station. NASA's space station will provide a suitable place where crews can work in orbit for as long as necessary. The shuttle will provide reliable, economic, routine round-trip transportation for the crews and supplies between Earth and orbit, serving the space station as both a taxicab and a truck.

The twentieth century, which began with history's first flight of a power-driven aircraft at Kitty Hawk, will very likely end with the first truly permanent orbital human habitat firmly established in space. The U.S. Space Station is scheduled to begin operations in the early 1990s. It promises to be an important legacy from us to the twenty-first century.

above: Space Camp's concept of the yet-to-be-built space station. Years away from being built, it's a reality at Space Camp where trainees relax after a hard day in the crew quarters.

right: One of NASA's proposed future space station modules being "manned" by a Space Camp trainee.

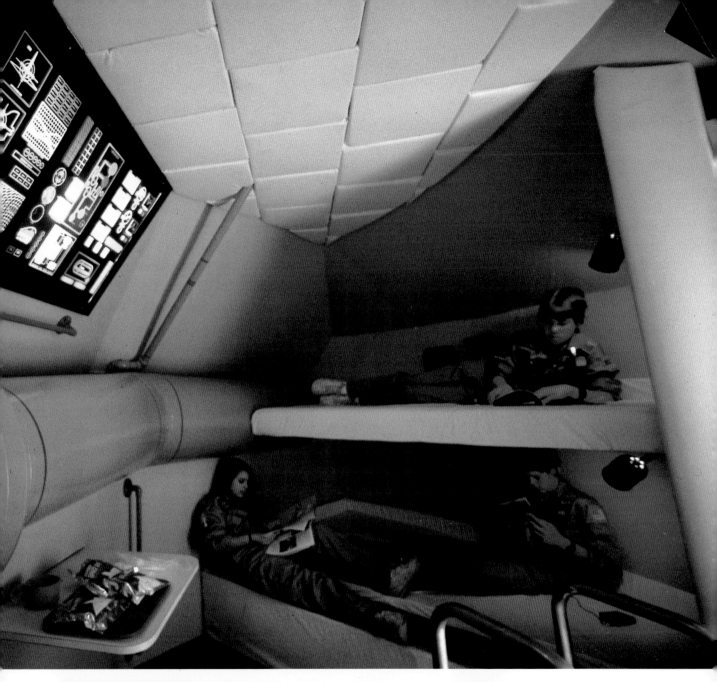

8.
Tomorrow and Beyond

Space Exploration in the Twenty-first Century

"Through a closer look at creation, we ought to gain a better knowledge of the Creator." These words were spoken by rocket scientist Wernher von Braun on the eve of the launch of Apollo 11 and Neil Armstrong's historic landing on the moon. Von Braun's dream of understanding our universe through space exploration is the same vision that has always motivated men and women to invent and to explore. Columbus dreamed this dream, as did Magellan and Byrd and Cook. It is the dream to know the unknown—the unknowable. As long as there are mysteries to unravel, mankind will search for answers.

In a geographic, if not an intellectual sense, space is indeed our last frontier. Already it appears within the realm of the possible—even probable—that some of you will inhabit colonies in space. The National Commission on Space, appointed by President Reagan, has submitted a phased development program that envisions human settlement on the moon by 2017 and on Mars by 2027.

This ambitious program involves an evolu-

tion of permanent, modular space facilities, beginning with the initial space station in low Earth orbit and rapidly moving to a space port in low orbit, a variable-gravity research laboratory, a network of space ports between Earth, moon and Mars, and ultimately, permanent bases on the moon and Mars.

While some of you will pioneer these settlements in space, many more of you will be involved here on Earth in developing the new equipment and technology that will be needed. The initial stages of the program calls for the creation of a "Highway to Space," which will require an extensive array of equipment, including three new transporters: a low-orbit cargo vehicle by the year 2000, a passenger vehicle and a "workhorse" transfer ship similar to the shuttle to carry both people and cargo beyond the moon and provide ferry service in the inner solar system. These vehicles are to be operational within fifteen years. An earth-orbital space port will follow the already planned space station. Next, a second fully manned and operational space port will be built on the moon.

All these elements will combine to enable us to move toward a twenty-first century "Bridge Between Worlds" and human habitation throughout the inner solar system.

In the five years from 2000 to 2005, the

left: Space Camp Mission Specialist Kelly Harrington looks toward her future as a commander/pilot of the space shuttle.

above: Mission Specialist Troy Adams in his EMU space suit outside Space Camp's orbiter Columbia.

top: NASA's concept of the future
Aerospace Plane.

above: Where we're headed: the planet
Venus.

above: Our home base: planet Earth.

top right: Mars photographed by
Viking I.

ACCESS TO THE INNER SOLAR SYSTEM

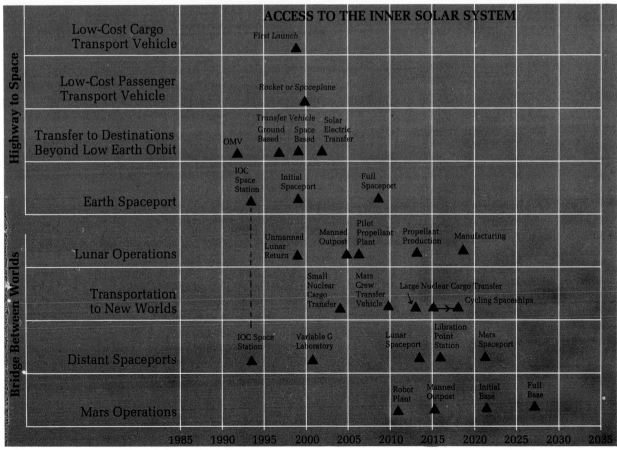

Highway to Space

- **Low-Cost Cargo Transport Vehicle** — First Launch (▲ ~1995)
- **Low-Cost Passenger Transport Vehicle** — Rocket or Spaceplane (▲ ~2000)
- **Transfer to Destinations Beyond Low Earth Orbit** — OMV (▲ ~1992); Transfer Vehicle: Ground Based (▲ ~1997), Space Based (▲ ~1999); Solar Electric Transfer (▲ ~2001)
- **Earth Spaceport** — IOC Space Station (▲ ~1993); Initial Spaceport (▲ ~1998); Full Spaceport (▲ ~2006)

Bridge Between Worlds

- **Lunar Operations** — Unmanned Lunar Return (▲ ~1996); Manned Outpost (▲ ~2003); Pilot Propellant Plant (▲ ~2005); Propellant Production (▲ ~2012); Manufacturing (▲ ~2017)
- **Transportation to New Worlds** — Small Nuclear Cargo Transfer (▲ ~2000); Mars Crew Transfer Vehicle (▲ ~2007); Large Nuclear Cargo Transfer (▲ ~2012); Cycling Spaceships (▲ ~2015)
- **Distant Spaceports** — IOC Space Station (▲ ~1993); Variable G Laboratory (▲ ~1999); Lunar Spaceport (▲ ~2011); Libration Point Station (▲ ~2014); Mars Spaceport (▲ ~2020)
- **Mars Operations** — Robot Plant (▲ ~2011); Manned Outpost (▲ ~2015); Initial Base (▲ ~2021); Full Base (▲ ~2027)

1985 1990 1995 2000 2005 2010 2015 2020 2025 2030 2035

bridge between worlds would support initial robotic lunar-surface operations, followed by a permanent outpost to support manned operations. Within ten more years, the space bridge would be extended to Mars for detailed robotic exploration, followed by a Mars outpost for human activity.

The lunar space port would be the launching point for a series of nuclear-powered cargo and crew-transfer vehicles that would shuttle to Mars on an increasingly active schedule. A third space port, located between the moon and Mars, would form the final stepping-stone on the way toward establishing a permanent space port on the "Red Planet."

Eventually, the moon and Mars outposts would become permanent installations that would furnish the necessities of life and sustain exploration, scientific investigation, resource development, prospecting, material processing and robotic fabrication. Rocket scientists believe that in the reduced gravity of the moon and Mars, we'll be able to send rockets farther into deep space than we can from Earth.

The catalogue of potential developments in space technology in the next fifty years reads like a Jules Verne novel. In some areas of technology, results already achieved by researchers in space suggest that whole new categories of products that will enrich our life on Earth can be created in a weightless environment.

Consider just these few examples.

Perfect crystals of many different types can be grown in space, free of pollution and undistorted by the stress of gravitational pull. These crystals can then be used to make microcircuits and other electronic components that are accurate and precise to a degree that we cannot match with crystals grown on Earth.

Whole new classes of chemical and pharmaceutical products might become possible because weightlessness, for the first time, will allow the necessary component elements to be mixed together with absolute consistency.

left: Halley's Comet returns to our Solar System every 76 years. This photo was taken by Jet Propulsion Laboratory astronomer Eleanor Helin with the 48-inch Schmidt telescope at Caltech's Palomar Observatory. It shows for the first time the full range of features characteristic of a well-developed ion tail.

below left: The spectacular rings of Saturn.

below: Spherical halo of neutrinos around Milky Way Galaxy emitting in light. A NASA scientist at the Laboratory for High Energy Astrophysics at the Goddard Space Flight Center has found possible new evidence suggesting that the subatomic particles known as neutrinos have mass, and that our galaxy may be surrounded by countless trillions that were produced during the first few moments of creation.

Alloys blending heretofore impossible combinations can be created in weightlessness. Once free of the pull of gravity, materials of different densities can be blended together, which is not possible on Earth. Therefore, it is theoretically possible to create an alloy of glass and copper or, by blowing gases into molten metal, to produce a foamlike titanium material that is both ultralight and ultrastrong.

In addition to making effective and creative use of the zero-gravity environment, other, parallel programs also will take place. The odds are great that you'll be able to contribute to the development of such programs as these.

The generation of enough electric power to supply all the Earth's needs by enormous arrays of solar cells in geosynchronous orbit.

The creation of totally new high-performance electric propulsion systems, including ion propulsion and mass-driver reaction engines run by propellants mined on Earth's moon and the moons of Mars.

Building and operating a robotic lunar prospector that will be able to examine the entire surface of the moon from low orbit, using remote sensors to examine polar craters.

Planning and mounting a mission to Mars to collect and return geological samples by early in the first decade of the twenty-first century.

Establishing a continuing program to test, optimize and demonstrate chemical engineering methods for separating materials found in space into pure elements suitable as raw materials for propellants and for manufacturing.

Participating in the continually accelerating research in construction and manufacture of space materials.

Designing, building and operating self-sustaining biospheres. These will be closed ecological "greenhouses" that are independent of Earth. Eventually they would reduce the need for long supply lines to our outposts on the moon and Mars.

The projects we have discussed represent only

left: When man goes to Mars, this could be how it will look. Overhead are several solar-sail-powered interplanetary shuttles. They've landed two manned capsules, various robot rovers and processors to mine and study the Martian surface. Before astronauts would arrive, a nuclear power station would also be landed for a five-year mission by a crew.

below left: Photograph of the landscape of Mars taken by *Mariner 9.*

a small sampling of the advances we will see as we enter our next dimension of space exploration. Man's reach has always exceeded his grasp. We have always envisioned challenges for ourselves that have been technically impossible at the time we conceived them. Then, with our uniquely human combination of unfettered imagination, dogged persistence and plain practicality, we have figured out ways to get the job done.

While we look with awe at the projects that have already been imagined, we cannot even contemplate those yet to be imagined. But we know that *imagined* they will be, and once we can hold a concept in our mind, it is only a matter of time before we make it a reality.

Finding our way to distant planets and developing the potential of space will be an enormous human endeavor, demanding vast resources of skill, dedication and courage from everyone who participates.

In the process, we will change the whole nature of our species . . . truly transforming ourselves from an Earth-bound to a space-faring people. The opportunities are there if you wish to grasp them—if you choose to be part of our future in space.

NASA

Glossary

Here is a list of words, abbreviations and acronyms commonly used by astronauts, other NASA personnel and the training staff at Space Camp. It's important for you to become familiar with these words because everyone connected with the space program uses this verbal shorthand constantly, almost as a second language.

Abort
To cut the mission or activity short. An abort can be called by the launch director, flight director or the commander if anything serious goes wrong during the flight.

Abort Advisory Check
This is a standard check prior to lift-off to make sure that the abort warning system is working properly.

Airlock
This is the small chamber that connects the flight deck and mid-deck of the orbiter with the Spacelab module, and it also serves as the exit for EVAs and the connector for docking with space stations. In the Space Camp simulations, astronauts performing an EVA will exit from the suit room into the work area.

Altitude
The shuttle's vertical distance from the surface of the Earth. The altitude is reported during launch and also in reporting the height of the shuttle's orbit.

Angle of Attack
The position of the shuttle when entering the atmosphere. On reentry the nose is pointed up at about 28 to 38 degrees (pitch) for atmospheric entry. Any higher angle of attack would cause the shuttle to skip off the Earth's atmosphere, and a lower angle of attack would cause the shuttle to burn up on reentry.

AOA
Abort Once Around. A mode of abort that involves a landing after nearly one orbit.

AOS
Acquisition of Signal. This is the point where air-to-ground communications resume after a loss of signal.

APU
Auxiliary Power Unit. The orbiter has three of these that are used to generate hydraulic power for the shuttle's rudder, wings and landing gear.

ATO
Abort To Orbit. A mode of abort that takes the orbiter into a lower-than-planned Earth orbit.

Auto-sequencer
Computer controller of the countdown. At T − 25 seconds the flight director switches total control of the launch over to the auto-sequencer.

Bearing
The compass direction in which the orbiter is traveling.

Cargo
The total complement of payload (one or more) on any one flight. It includes everything contained in the orbiter cargo bay plus other equipment, hardware and consumables located elsewhere in the orbiter that are user-unique and are not carried as part of the basic orbit payload support.

Cargo Bay
The unpressurized mid-part of the orbiter fuselage, behind the cabin bulkhead where most payloads are carried. Its maximum usable payload envelope is 15 feet in diameter and 60 feet long.

Commander
This crew member has ultimate responsibility for the safety of embarked personnel and has authority throughout the flight to deviate from the flight plan, procedures, and personnel assignments as necessary to preserve crew safety or vehicle integrity. The commander is also responsible for the overall execution of the flight plan in compliance with NASA policy, mission rules and Mission Control Center directives.

DAP
Digital Auto Pilot. An automatic system used to maintain a specific course or attitude in orbit.

Deorbit Burn
An OMS burn used to slow the shuttle down for reentry.

Deployment
The process of removing a payload from a towed or berthed position in the cargo bay and releasing that payload to a position free of the orbiter.

Depress or Depressurize
The act of releasing the atmosphere out of a container. Usually it refers to preparations to open an airlock prior to an EVA.

Dock/Undock
The process of attaching to or detaching from another object in space, most often a space station or other spacecraft.

ECLSS
Environmental Control and Life Support System. The system that supplies air and water and maintains air pressure in the crew cabin.

EMU
The Extravehicular Mobility Unit (space suit) is a self-contained (no umbilicals) life-support system and anthropomorphic pressure garment for use by crew members during ExtraVehicular Activity. It provides thermal and micrometeoroid protection.

ESA
The European Space Agency is an international organization acting on behalf of its member states (Belgium, Denmark, France, Federal Republic of Germany, Italy, the Netherlands, Spain, Sweden, Switzerland, and the United Kingdom). The ESA directs a European industrial team responsible for the development and manufacture of Spacelab.

ET
The external tank of the shuttle that carries liquid oxygen and hydrogen for the main engines on launch.

ET Sep
External Tank Separation. The point after main engine cut-off when the external tank is released from the orbiter and the giant tank tumbles into the atmosphere and burns up.

EVA
ExtraVehicular Activity. A common NASA term for space-walks and other journeys outside the protection of the spacecraft.

5DF (Five-D-F)
Five Degrees of Freedom. A device that helps simulate weightlessness. In your simulated missions the astronauts will often work inside a 5DF during EVAs.

Flare
Pitching the orbiter nose-up on landing. This maneuver helps change the glide slope from 22 degrees to less than 2.

GAS
GetAway Special. A small self-contained payload housed in cylindrical containers in the cargo bay.

Gear
1. The landing gear of the orbiter. 2. Equipment used in experiments or other activities.

G-Force
The unit of measurement of gravitational pull. One g is the force of Earth's normal gravity. Two g's is twice this force, etc.

Glide Slope
The angle of the shuttle's descent to the Earth.

Go
A term granting permission to proceed with an activity.

H_2 (aitch-two)
Hydrogen. It is used in liquid form to power the main engines and the power generators on the shuttle.

HAC
Heading Alignment Cylinder. An imaginary circle or cylinder in front of and just to one side of the runway. On final approach, the orbiter flies around a portion of this circle until it is correctly aligned with the runway entry point.

HUT
Hard Upper Torso. The fiberglass shell in the upper torso of the space suit.

Hydraulic Pressure
Pressure produced by the APUs used to power the landing gear and control surfaces of the orbiter on launch and landing. If pressure is too low, the equipment will not function properly.

Ignition
The point when an engine or rocket starts combustion.

Inclination
The angle of an orbit relative to the equator.

Ionization
The buildup of ions around the orbiter as it reenters the Earth's atmosphere. Often a red glow is seen around the shuttle as the ionization buildup occurs.

Ionization Blackout
When ionization builds up it blocks out all radio communication with the orbiter, causing a temporary LOS.

IVA
IntraVehicular Activity. Work and operations performed inside the spacecraft.

Joystick
The control in front of the commander and pilot used to move the orbiter. Only one of the two can control the joystick at any one time.

Launch Control
The room where the launch is supervised. Generally this is a separate facility from Mission Control, either at Kennedy Space Center or at Vandenberg Air Force Base.

Launch Pad
The area at which the stacked space shuttle undergoes final prelaunch checkout and countdown, and from which it is launched.

Lift-Off
The point when the space shuttle moves up off the launch pad.

LOS
Loss of Signal. This occurs when the orbiting spacecraft moves out of range of Earth-based or space-based communications. With the addition of the TDRSS satellites the amount of LOS during the typical mission has been greatly reduced.

LOX
Liquid Oxygen. Used as fuel in the ET and the orbiter.

Mach (1, 2, 3, etc.)
The speed of sound. Mach 2 is double the speed of sound and Mach 3 is triple, etc.

Mains
Short for Main Engines.

Maneuver
Moving a spacecraft or other object.

Max Q
Period of maximum aerodynamic pressure on the orbiter during a typical launch.

MECO
Main Engine CutOff. This occurs usually when the orbiter is at the right altitude and is traveling fast enough to achieve its proper orbit.

Microgravity
A more precise scientific term for weightlessness or zero g (qv), which recognizes the fact that very small gravitational forces actually are present in an orbiter or other vehicle in space, although the astronauts may not be able to feel them.

Mission
The performance of a coherent set of investigations or operations in space to achieve program goals. A single mission might require more than one flight, or more than one mission might be accomplished on a single flight.

Mission Control
The center where all operations of the orbiter are coordinated during the mission. It is often referred to as Houston.

Mission Specialist

This crew member is responsible for coordination of overall payload/STS interaction and, during the payload operations phase, directs the allocation of the STS and crew resources to the accomplishment of the combined payload objectives. The mission specialist will have prime responsibility for experiments to which no payload specialist is assigned, and/or will assist the payload specialist when appropriate.

MMU

Manned Maneuvering Unit. A personal spacecraft used to catch disabled satellites and move astronauts around to make repairs.

NASA

National Aeronautics and Space Administration. The agency established by the federal government in 1957 with primary responsibility for the U.S. space program.

NBS

Neutral Buoyancy Simulator. A very large pool in which the buoyancy of water is used to simulate weightlessness for purposes of training and experimentation.

Newton

The unit of force required to give a mass of one kilogram an acceleration of one meter-per-second squared.

Nominal

This means that the performance of a device or activity is within the standards set prior to the mission. In other words, things are normal.

OMS (rhymes with homes)

Orbital Maneuvering Subsystem. The two engines on the orbiter used to lower or heighten its orbit during a mission. It is used to slow the orbiter down for reentry.

Orbit

When a spacecraft continuously circles the Earth in space.

Orbiter

The principal part of the shuttle. It carries the crew and payload.

"Other Side of the Hill"

An expression used describing the acquisition of signal after a loss of signal.

O_2 (oh-two)

Oxygen.

"Over the Hill"

An expression describing an upcoming loss of signal.

Pallet

An unpressurized platform, designed for installation in the orbiter cargo bay, for mounting instruments and equipment requiring direct space exposure.

Payload

The total complement of specific instruments, space equipment, support hardware and consumables carried in the orbiter to accomplish a discrete activity in space.

Payload Specialist

This crew member, who may or may not be a career astronaut, is responsible for the operation and management of the experiments or other payload elements that are assigned to him or her, and for the achievement of their objectives. The payload specialist will be an expert in experiment design and operation.

PI

Principle Investigator. Research scientist who is in charge of the conduct of an experiment carried by any STS element.

Pilot

This crew member is second in command of the flight and assists the commander as required in the conduct of all phases of orbiter flight.

Pitch

Up/Down rotation of the nose of the craft.

PLSS

Primary Life Support System. The backpack portion of the space suit that supplies oxygen, suit pressurization and ventilation and that cools the water used to maintain body temperature.

POCC

Payload Operations Control Center. Control center for Spacelab payloads.

Power Up/Down

Term used to describe activation and deactivation of equipment and instruments.

Press to MECO

This is the call from Mission Control to the shuttle telling the crew they can continue to main engine cutoff (MECO) even if one or two of the main engines fail.

Range

The horizontal distance between two objects. In the shuttle program it is used to describe the distance of the orbiter from the launch pad after lift-off, and also to describe the distance between the orbiter and other objects, such as the space station.

RCS

Reaction Control System. This is a series of thrusters in various locations around the orbiter used for maneuvering in space.

Retrieval

The process of utilizing the Remote Manipulator System and/or other handling aids to return a captured payload to a stowed or berthed position. No payload is considered retrieved until it is fully stowed for safe return or berthed for repair and maintenance tasks.

RHC

Rotational Hand Controller. Joystick-type device used to fly the orbiter.

RMS

Remote Manipulator System. The robot arm on the shuttle.

Roger

A word used to confirm that the message is received.

Roll
Rotation around the axis from the nose to the tail.

RTLS
Return to Launch Site. A mode of abort that requires a turn-around and return to the launch site for landing.

Simulator
The heavily computer-dependent training facility that imitates flight hardware responses.

Spacelab
An orbiting laboratory, developed by NASA and the European Space Agency (ESA), that can fly a variety of different experiments. Your Spacelab simulator is virtually identical to the crew trainer used at Marshall Space Flight Center.

Space Shuttle
Orbiter, external tank and solid rocket boosters.

Speed Brake
The rudder on the orbiter is split down the middle and when the speed brake is activated the two halves fan out and help slow the spacecraft down with extra drag during the landing approach.

Sputnik
The first artificial satellite launched by the Soviet Union in October 1957.

SRB
Solid Rocket Boosters. The two slender rockets strapped to the side of the orbiter and ET that give the shuttle immediate power at lift-off and burn up all their fuel in just two minutes.

SRB Sep
The point when the boosters separate from the rest of the shuttle. The boosters fall back to Earth and are recovered in the ocean to be reused.

SSCP
Small self-contained payload. See GAS.

SSME
Space Shuttle Main Engines. The shuttle has three of these on the base of the orbiter. They burn hydrogen and oxygen from the ET.

Stow/Unstow
The act of taking out or putting away gear or equipment.

STS
The Space Transportation System. An integrated system consisting of the space shuttle (orbiter, external tank, solid rocket boosters and flight kits), upper stages, Spacelab and any associated flight hardware and software.

S-Turn
A maneuver performed four times during atmospheric entry to help slow the orbiter down before landing.

Suit Up
The procedure for putting on a space suit.

TAEM
Terminal Area Energy Management. One of the final portions of the orbiter's landing sequence, in which the vehicle is flown so it will arrive at the landing area at precisely the right speed and altitude.

TAL (rhymes with pal)
Trans-Atlantic Landing. This is an abort procedure used when it is no longer possible to return to the launch site (RTLS), but the shuttle has sufficient altitude to make it to Daker, West Africa.

TDRSS (tee-dress)
Tracking and Data Relay Satellite System. NASA's new link for communications and space travel. Using TDRSS most shuttle flights can remain in contact with the ground more than 80 percent of the time in orbit.

Thrust
The forward force produced in reaction to the escaping gases in jet propulsion.

Velcro
Space-age material used plentifully in space to secure objects, especially cue cards, in place in zero gravity.

Velocity
The shuttle's relative speed to the Earth.

Yaw
The rotation of the spacecraft on an axis going vertically through the middle of the ship.

Zero-Gravity
The condition of apparent weightlessness encountered in orbit and during many other portions of a space flight.

Appendix

For more information on space and space-related careers.

Space Camp

Send applications to: United States Space Camp, The Space and Rocket Center, Tranquility Base, Huntsville, AL 35807.

NASA Education Offices

If you know the title of a specific NASA publication that you want, you can order it from: Superintendent of Documents, Government Printing Office, Washington, DC 20402.

Other inquiries may be directed to the Educational Office at the NASA Center that serves your state.

NASA Ames Research Center, Moffett Field, CA 94035. Serves Alaska, Arizona, California, Hawaii, Idaho, Montana, Nevada, Oregon, Utah, Washington and Wyoming.

NASA Goddard Space Flight Center, Greenbelt, MD 20771. Serves Connecticut, Delaware, District of Columbia, Maine, Maryland, Massachusetts, New Hampshire, New Jersey, New York, Pennsylvania, Rhode Island and Vermont.

NASA Johnson Space Center, Houston, TX 77058. Serves Colorado, Kansas, Nebraska, New Mexico, North Dakota, Oklahoma, South Dakota and Texas.

NASA Kennedy Space Center, Kennedy Space Center, FL 32899. Serves Florida, Georgia, Puerto Rico and the U.S. Virgin Islands.

NASA Langley Research Center, Langley Station, Hampton, VA 23665. Serves Kentucky, North Carolina, South Carolina, Virginia and West Virginia.

NASA Lewis Research Center, 21000 Brookpark Road, Cleveland, OH 44135. Serves Illinois, Indiana, Michigan, Minnesota, Ohio and Wisconsin.

NASA Marshall Space Flight Center, Marshall Space Flight Center, AL 35812. Serves Alabama, Arkansas, Iowa, Louisiana, Mississippi, Missouri and Tennessee.

Museums

National Air and Space Museum, Education Department, Sixth Street and Independence Avenue, Washington, DC 20560.

The Space and Rocket Center, Teacher Resource Center, Huntsville, AL 35807.

Career Information

Aerospace and Aviation

ALPA Occupational Guides, Air Line Pilots Association, 1329 E Street, N.W., Washington, DC 20004.

Aerospace Education Foundation, 1750 Pennsylvania Avenue, N.W., Washington, DC 20006.

The Aerospace Medical Association, Washington National Airport, Washington, DC 20001.

Aerospace Industries Association, 1725 DeSales Street, N.W., Washington, DC 20036.

Aerospace Youth Council, 1785 Massachusetts Avenue, N.W., Washington, DC 20036.

American Institute of Aeronautics and Astronautics, 1290 Avenue of the Americas, New York, NY 10019.

Aviation Technical Education Council, P.O. Box 51133, Tulsa, OK 74151.

Flight Engineers International Association, 905 Sixteenth Street, N.W., Washington, DC 20006.

General Aviation Manufacturers Association, Suite 1200-A, 1205 Connecticut Ave., N.W., Washington, DC 20036.

National Aeronautic Association, Room 610, 806 15th Street, N.W., Washington, DC 20005.

National Aerospace Education Association, Shoreham Building, 806 15th Street, N.W., Washington, DC 20005.

National Defense Transportation Association, 1612 K Street, N.W., Washington, DC 20006.

Young Astronaut Council, P.O. Box 65432, Washington, DC 20036.

Engineering

American Institute of Chemical Engineers, 345 East 47th Street, New York, NY 10017.

American Institute of Industrial Engineers, 25 Technology Park, Atlanta, GA 30071.

American Society of Certified Engineering Technicians, 2029 K Street, N.W., Washington, DC 20006.

American Society for Engineering Education, Suite 400, One Dupont Circle, Washington, DC 20036.

American Society of Mechanical Engineers, 345 East 47th Street, New York, NY 10006.

American Society for Metals, Metals Park, OH 44073.

American Society for Quality Control, 161 West Wisconsin Avenue, Milwaukee, WI 53203.

Biomedical Engineering Directory, AIBS/BIAC, 3900 Wisconsin Avenue, N.W., Washington, DC 20016.

Consulting Engineers Council of the USA, 1155 15th Street, N.W., Washington, DC 20005.

Electronic Industries Association, 2001 I Street, N.W., Washington, DC 20017.

Engineering Manpower Commission, 345 East 47th Street, New York, NY 10017.

Engineers Council for Professional Development, 345 East 47th Street, New York, NY 10017.

Institute of Electrical and Electronic Engineers, Inc., 345 East 47th Street, New York, NY 10017.

Junior Engineering Technical Society, 345 East 47th Street, New York, NY 10017.

National Machine Tool Builders Association, 7901 Westpark Drive, McLean, VA 22101.

National Society of Professional Engineers, 2029 K Street, N.W., Washington, DC 20006.

Scientific Apparatus Makers Association, 370 Lexington Avenue, New York, NY 10017.

Society of Photographic Scientists and Engineers, 1330 Massachusetts Avenue, N.W., Washington, DC 20005.

Society of Women Engineers, 345 East 47th Street, New York, NY 10017.

Science & Mathematics

American Academy for the Advancement of Science, 1776 Massachusetts Avenue, N.W., Washington, DC 20036.

American Astronomical Society, 211 Fitz Randolph Road, Princeton, NJ 08540.

American Geological Institute, 2001 M Street, N.W., Washington, DC 20037.

American Geophysical Union, 2100 Pennsylvania Avenue, N.W., Washington, DC 20037.

American Institute of Biological Sciences, 3900 Wisconsin Avenue, N.W., Washington, DC 20016.

American Institute of Physics, 335 East 45th Street, New York, NY 10017.

American Meteorological Society, 45 Beacon Street, Boston, MA 02108.

American Society for Microbiology, 1913 I Street, N.W., Washington, DC 20006.

Association of American Geographers, 1710 16th Street, N.W., Washington, DC 20009.

Ecological Society of America, Department of Botany, University of North Carolina, Chapel Hill, NC 27514.

Federation of Americans Supporting Science and Technology, 1785 Massachusetts Avenue, N.W., Washington, DC 20036.

Institute of Environmental Sciences, 940 East Northwest Highway, Mt. Prospect, IL 60056.

Manufacturing Chemists Association, 1825 Connecticut Avenue, N.W., Washington, DC 20009.

Mathematical Association of America, 1225 Connecticut Avenue, N.W., Washington, DC 20036.

National Environmental Health Association, 1600 Pennsylvania Street, Denver, CO 80203.

National Oceanography Association, 1900 L Street, N.W., Washington, DC 20036.

National Science Teachers Association, 1742 Connecticut Avenue, N.W., Washington, DC 20009.

Society for Industrial and Applied Mathematics, 33 South 17th Street, Philadelphia, PA 19103.

Society of Exploration Geophysics, Box 3098, Tulsa, OK 74101.

Information & Data Handling

American Federation of Information Processing Societies, 1815 North Lynn Street, Arlington, VA 22209.

Association for Systems Management, 24587 Bagley Road, Cleveland, OH 44138.

Federal Communications Commission, 1919 M Street, N.W., Washington, DC 20554.

Institute for Certification of Computer Professionals, Suite 2828, 35 East Wacker Drive, Chicago, IL 60601.

Military Aviation

U.S. Air Force

Air Force Academy: During your junior year of high school, and after January 31, write the Registrar (RRSS), United States Air Force Academy, Colorado Springs, CO 80840-5651.

Air Force ROTC: Write to AFROTC/RROO, Maxwell Air Force Base, AL 36112-6663, or contact the Professor of Aerospace Studies at the college you wish to attend.

Officer Training School: Write HQ USAF Recruiting Service (RSAANE), Randolph Air Force Base, TX 78150-5421.

U.S. Navy

Naval Academy: Write Superintendent, United States Naval Academy, Annapolis, MD 21402, ATTN: Director of Candidate Guidance.

NROTC and Officer Training: Write Navy Opportunity Information Center, P.O. Box 5000, Clifton, NJ 07015-5000.

U.S. Marine Corps

Officer Training: Write Marine Corps Opportunities, P.O. Box 38901, Los Angeles, CA 90038.

Mission Reports (Scientific & Technical)

These are potential sources of items and information from independent contractors who have been involved in space technology and experimentation. Prior to ordering any materials, a determination should be made of availability, price and time required for delivery.

National Technical Information Service, 5285 Port Royal Road, Springfield, VA 22151.

Scientific & Technical Information Facility, 800 Elkridge Landing Road, Linthicum Heights, MD 21090.

GetAway Special Payloads

These small self-contained payloads, called GAS projects, fall into two separate categories. In the first, corporations, universities and other scientific researchers pay a fee to have their projects carried into space. In the second category, called Project Explorer, certain student experiments will be carried into space at no cost.

For Project Explorer experiments, contact Konrad K. Dannenberg, Consultant, c/o United States Space Camp, The Space and Rocket Center, Tranquility Base, Huntsville, AL 35807.

For commercial experiments, contact Space Transportation System Utilization, National Aeronautics and Space Administration, Washington, DC 20546.